W9-AIA-801

3.

SAD

IS

NOT

BAD

IT'S HOW WE GRIEVE
AFTER WE'VE LOVED

BY HARRIET VOGEL

outskirtspress

DENVER, COLORADO

The opinions expressed in this manuscript are solely the opinions of the author and do not represent the opinions or thoughts of the publisher. The author has represented and warranted full ownership and/or legal right to publish all the materials in this book.

Sad Is Not Bad
It's How We Grieve After We've Loved
Copyright © 2016 Harriet Vogel
v4.0 R1.0

Cover Photo © 2016 Harriet Vogel . All rights reserved - used with permission.

This book may not be reproduced, transmitted, or stored in whole or in part by any means, including graphic, electronic, or mechanical without the express written consent of the publisher except in the case of brief quotations embodied in critical articles and reviews.

Outskirts Press, Inc.
http://www.outskirtspress.com

ISBN: 978-1-4787-5895-2

Outskirts Press and the "OP" logo are trademarks belonging to Outskirts Press, Inc.

PRINTED IN THE UNITED STATES OF AMERICA

"Loss is our legacy

Insight is our gift

Memory is our guide"

Hope Edelman
Motherless Daughters

For Jane,
I hope reading
this helps you
gain insight into
grieving Norman's
death and living
life as you
travel the "journey
of grief.

Harriet Vogel
7/19

TABLE OF CONTENTS

FOREWORD i

INTRODUCTION iii

PREFACE viii

SHIVA 1

HIGH HOLY DAYS 36

THANKSGIVING / CHANUKAH 67

VALENTINE'S DAY 100

PASSOVER / UNVEILING 138

SHAVUOT / FATHER'S DAY 167

YAHRZEIT 199

SECOND YEAR BEGINS 234

EPILOGUE 245

GLOSSARY 254

ACKNOWLEDGEMENTS 262

JERRY'S HOROSCOPE 12/14/36 264

FOREWORD

I have had the pleasure of working with Harriet Vogel for many years as a colleague and friend while employed as a hospice bereavement coordinator. She has actively participated as a group facilitator for spouses, adult children, parents and children who have suffered losses. Harriet has the gift of being a guide and a "listening presence" assisting those in grief on their healing journey.

When Jerry, her husband of forty-five years, died suddenly, she found herself on her own grief journey. Having learned much from the bereaved, Harriet realized she must find her own way to healing her intense loss and pain. She turned to something familiar, the letter writing part of Marriage Encounter that she and Jerry had utilized throughout their marriage to help them through both challenging and memorable times.

When she was ready, following the shock, disbelief, and denial associated with the sudden death of a loved one, she began writing letters to Jerry to describe the myriad of feelings, thoughts, ups and downs of her ever-changing journey through the "river of grief". Sometimes the river became a tsunami of loss, memories, fear, loneliness and past joy as well. Harriet's book is a compilation of these letters and has been written to help others who are experiencing their own journey of grief and loss from the death of a loved person. It is her personal journey through loss but it is also the universal journey we all experience when confronted by death.

This book is a gift of understanding, of caring and compassion written and shared by an extraordinary woman whose desire is to be a guide, helpmate, and companion to those whose lives have been impacted by the loss of a loved one. She accomplishes that task with sincerity, love and compassion; the beautiful hallmarks of my dear friend and colleague. I am honored to have been asked to write this foreword for her.

Sincerely,

Cathleen Fanslow, MA, RN, CNS author of:

Using The Power Of Hope To Cope With Dying;
The Four Stages Of Hope.

INTRODUCTION

On August 30, 2005 my husband Jerry died suddenly from a heart attack; he was "only" 68 years old. Married 45 years, we liked to say we had 50 together as we met and dated on and off from 1955 until we married in 1960. The week of Thanksgiving of 2004, we actually took the family (our three sons, their wives and the six grandchildren) on vacation to celebrate those 50 years, as well as my upcoming 65th birthday, our eldest son Craig's 40th birthday, and our youngest grandchild Grant's first birthday. Had it been planned for the following year, we never would have experienced it. It will remain as a Thanksgiving to remember for us all.

Jerry was an insulin dependent diabetic for 40 years. From the beginning of his diagnosis I knew he might die of a heart attack or suffer another debilitating side effect of diabetes. Seventeen years prior to his death, he had a major heart attack leaving him with only one healthy artery supporting his heart. I also thought it was probable that he would die first. However, no matter how many times I might have considered that probability, I experienced my husband's death as sudden and traumatic.

As a grief counselor for over 18 years in two hospice agencies and private practice, as well as experiencing other deaths of close family and friends, I have learned that even when someone is terminally ill for an extended time, the death may seem 'sudden'. It just might be the trauma of receiving the phone call informing you of the death or when one has to make a decision to remove life support, or it might be that moment when the reality of a loved one's impending death hits the heart versus the head. These moments can trigger intense grief reactions, such as sobbing, screaming, fainting or anything related to being in shock; the same reactions associated with a sudden, traumatic death. I firmly believe that every death on some level is sudden and traumatic – Jerry's was.

Soon after Jerry's death I began writing letters to him. We had a long history of communicating and sharing in that way, starting when Jerry went into the army during our dating years. I wrote long, detailed letters and he wrote back when he could, keeping the relationship going even though we were physically apart.

In 1974 we went on a Marriage Encounter Weekend, a retreat experience where together, along with other couples we learned the skill of writing letters to one's spouse, sharing our feelings as an effective means of improving our loving relationship. I recall using the acronym "C-C-C" for this "Crash Course in Communication". Afterward, we joined several couples in our community and established a monthly meeting. Following the guidelines established on that initial weekend, we continued to meet for over thirty years. Through this discipline Jerry and I deepened our love, friendship, and trust to be totally open with one another. We also used this technique with our growing family and the practice of writing feelings led to an ease of sharing feelings verbally for us all. For this gift of Marriage Encounter we had always been grateful.

In my work of supporting the bereaved as a hospice grief counselor beginning in 1991 and having a private practice since 2001, I have encouraged my clients to write letters to their deceased loved ones. For those who did try this "weird" idea of writing to a dead person, I have always heard of benefiting results. It assists in healing regrets or past hurts. Sometimes it merely is a trigger for releasing emotions. At other times it helps go deeper into one's feelings of grief. Writing always keeps the connection going even though it has changed. As expressed by Morrie Schwartz in the book *Tuesdays With Morrie,* "Death ends a life, not a relationship." We may need to let go of the body—but never the love.

After his death, I wrote Jerry letters for two years. This book is based on the first year only. Sometimes I wrote daily; sometimes many weeks separated one letter from the next. Without these written letters, I never would have been able to recall some of the experiences nor the feelings accompanying them. By writing and re-reading the letters, I have been able to trace my healing journey. I have come to see grief as a journey, with bumps along the way and sometimes forks in the road. I've often reminded my clients that they need to "wear a seat belt", at least for the first year, as we have very little control over the journey itself.

My personal experience became a validation of all I had learned as a professional counseling the bereaved. I learned that "sad is not bad" and that embracing one's emotions and reactions can lead to healing. It has worked for my clients and it has worked for me.

Within my letters the reader will find many references to Jewish ritual. A glossary can be found at the end of the book to help the reader understand the meaning of Hebrew words and phrases and gain a clearer understanding of Jewish rituals.

I have always believed that the Jewish rituals for death and dying, while formulated about two thousand years ago, are very realistic and relevant to what modern psychology teaches. In Judaism, it is believed that the death rituals support the mourner in facing the reality of death and helps them through the grief journey, and helps the souls of the deceased as well. According to Kabbalah, we are all souls who are in physical bodies and there is a need for the soul to transition. The funeral is one of the ways to help the soul work out their attachments to living people. As the mourners "say goodbye", it sends the soul love and helps the deceased and their loved ones with the separation. Just like a twisted Havdalah candle, we are all intertwined.

The Kaddish, the traditional prayer for the dead, is interactive between griever and soul. While there is no reference to death in this ancient prayer, it is very powerful. "It keeps the living together and forms a bridge to the mysterious realm of the dead." (Page 622 *Gates of Prayer*)

These letters are only a sampling of the ones I wrote to Jerry. Sometimes I copied the letter verbatim and on occasion I modified it to allow for passage of time, to eliminate excessive dialogue, for the benefit of further exploration or to highlight an important message.

I share these letters with you in the hope that as you navigate your grief journey, you too will be able to feel your feelings, embrace them as a healing modality, and eventually integrate the death of your loved one into your life. The letters have been written to the best of my recollection. Some names have been changed.

I believe that a broken heart that has healed is a stronger heart.

Harriet Vogel

March 28, 2015

PREFACE

Tuesday, August 30th, 2005

On a typical summer evening, after work Jerry and I greeted each other at home with a hug and kiss. We shared a light, healthy dinner in our screened porch. On evenings like this we loved to sit outside together to eat, talk, and relax.

Shortly after the meal, Jerry told me he felt nauseous and was going into the house to rest. I cleaned up after our meal and straightened up the kitchen while he lay down.

When I checked on him a little while later, I found him still nauseous and beginning to sweat.

"I don't like the way you look," I said, peering at him in concern. He'd had these symptoms on and off over the weekend and the increase in his discomfort mirrored the early stages of his heart attack seventeen years prior.

"You're sweating now," I continued. "I think we need to go to the emergency room."

"No, no, no," he said quickly, insisting he was okay. "I'll just go upstairs and lie down and wait it out."

While I was not completely comfortable with his decision, I chose to respect it for the time being. He often 'waited it out' when he had imbalanced blood sugar related to his diabetes.

I just could not shake the feeling of concern growing within me, especially because of the previous weekend. We had been visiting with our dear friends Louise, David, Phoebe, and Ed in Louise and David's home in Massachusetts. Louise, Phoebe, Ed, and I set out to go kayaking while Jerry and David played golf. When we came back after our kayaking expedition, we were surprised to see the golfers had already returned; they were not expected back for a while.

"What are you doing here?" I asked Jerry in surprise. He was seated in a chair on the porch, just sitting there without any expression.

"He wasn't feeling well," David responded. "He was nauseous."

I peered at Jerry, alarmed by his listlessness and remembering how nausea and weakness preempted his heart attack in the past. Diabetics do not always feel pain when having a heart attack due to changes in their nervous system. The more common "pain in the chest" or "pain down the right arm" may not be experienced. Nausea and sweating are actually red flags for a possible heart attack.

"You really should go to the emergency room," I said.

Jerry shook his head. "No…"

"This is exactly what happened seventeen years ago when you had your heart attack," I reminded him, as my stomach began to tighten.

"I'll be fine," he assured me. "I just need to rest."

I suggested canceling the remainder of our plans for the day but Jerry insisted it was just a little upset stomach and that he would eat lightly at dinner. He made it through the meal and we went on to attend a concert at Tanglewood.

Upon arriving home from the concert the six of us stepped into the kitchen and spontaneously were drawn together forming a tight circle.

"It doesn't get better than this," said Louise not knowing that would be the very last time we shared a group hug.

The next morning, Sunday, he felt fine. He was joking around, his usual self, and was looking forward to Louise's delicious spread at brunch. We all enjoyed the meal together and then Jerry and I set off for home, stopping in Connecticut to visit our son Gary's family to say goodbye before our much-antici-pated trip to China in a few days.

Jerry was behind the wheel for the two-hour drive, seemingly having recovered from whatever was ailing him the day before. He easily climbed the stairs at Gary's house and rang the doorbell.

From inside the house came a flurry of hurried footsteps and then the door swung open to reveal our 21-month-old grandson, Grant.

A smile broke out over Grant's face as he yelled, "Gran pa!" in his enthusiastic, passionate way. Jerry absolutely lit up, a grin from ear to ear. When around the grandchildren and their incredible energy and as they climbed onto his lap for hugs and kisses, he often said, "This is what makes life worthwhile."

As we visited with our son Gary, his wife Shelley, 3½year old Allie, and young Grant, there was a sudden change in Jerry's physical demeanor. Instead of diving right into playing with the grandkids, he sat perched on a low stone wall, quieter than usual. After the visit, as we said our goodbyes at the door, hugs and kisses all around, I offered to drive. Gary's family stood in the doorframe, waving, as Jerry and I climbed into the car and started the engine.

Suddenly, Allie broke away from her parents and rushed down the stairs towards the car. She was moving very fast, almost hurrying, and her parents hurried after her, concerned. Jerry lowered the window and Allie was lifted up to give him a final kiss. I later wondered if Allie, deeply compassionate and intuitive from a very young age, sensed that something was not right.

The ride back to Long Island was uneventful. We started planning our annual Chanukah party in Florida and went to bed shortly after getting home.

Monday was work as usual for both of us and Jerry went to his weekly yoga class at night. While his symptoms came and went over the course of the weekend, their return on Tuesday evening made me very uncomfortable. I always respected Jerry's independence and his ability to control his diabetes regimen. However, that night, I noticed his symptoms worsening when I went up to check on him after an hour or so. He was lying in bed and did not look good.

"You're not getting any better, Jer," I said firmly. "I'm giving you a choice. Either you get in the car and allow me to take you to the Emergency Room or I'm calling 911."

I waited for his response, my anxiety growing, ready to spring into action. When he did not decide, I went around the bed, picked up the phone, and called for an ambulance.

A minute later, with help on the way, I returned to his side. His eyes were closed and he was still breathing but he was not responding when I spoke to him.

What do I do??? I need to open the door so the paramedics can get in...but how can I leave him right now?

Deeply in conflict, I ran downstairs as fast as I could, pulled the front door open, and rushed back up to Jerry. He was totally unresponsive and looked as though he was unconscious. I felt a sudden calm wash over me, perhaps shock, as I stood next to him, looking down at his slack expression.

"Hang in there, Jerry, hold on. Help is coming," I said. "I love you. I love you. I love you…"

I repeated those words over and over and then, in one of his final gifts to me, his lips parted and he slowly mouthed, "I love you," one meaningful last time.

The sound of sirens broke through the air and suddenly there was a commotion down in the foyer.

"We're upstairs!" I cried.

Two police officers hurried into the room. I stepped to the side so they could attend to Jerry as he suddenly opened his eyes and became very alert.

"So tell me what happened, Mr. Vogel?" one officer asked.

"I must have fallen asleep," Jerry replied normally, as though the events of the last few minutes had not taken place.

What was going on? Was that his sense of humor?

"What, are you kidding?" I interrupted. "That was no sleep."

It was baffling. Jerry actually seemed almost totally okay as the sound of running footsteps on the stairs brought firemen into the room as well. As they quickly set about opening their bags of medical equipment to examine him, the female police officer approached me.

"Would you mind coming downstairs to answer a few questions?"

"Sure," I replied. I felt reassured and comfortable between Jerry's sudden recovery and the paramedics monitoring him. The officer and I went into the kitchen and I answered the usual questions about Jerry's date of birth and health history and recounted what had led to my calling for help.

Afterward, I was surprised to see Jerry standing in the living room, fully dressed.

"Ma'am, I just want you to know that he dressed himself and walked down the stairs on his own," the male officer said to me as Jerry climbed onto a gurney unassisted. A rush of relief washed over me.

One of the paramedics approached Jerry with an oxygen mask. Jerry had a fear of medical masks being placed over his face, stemming from a traumatic childhood tonsillectomy, and quickly said, "You are not putting that on my face. If you do, we'll really have a problem here!" Everyone burst out laughing at his joking demeanor but I knew how serious he was about his old phobia.

"Would you like to go in the ambulance with him, ma'am?"

How will we get home? I thought, assuming that Jerry would be released from the hospital by morning.

"No, thank you," I replied. "I'll follow in my own car. I know where the hospital is." I felt confident as I made that decision. Jerry was up, alert, in good spirits, talking and joking as he usually did, moving around independently, and was in good hands.

My drive to the hospital was quiet. It was late and the roads were empty. As I drove, I contemplated different ways I could go to get to the hospital as quickly as possible, though I was much calmer and confident now that Jerry was okay. I had even remembered to take my knitting with me as I anticipated a long night in the emergency room.

What I did not anticipate was that Jerry died in the ambulance en route to the hospital, a mere 2 miles from our home.

I arrived at the hospital around 11 PM. The waiting room was empty as I filled out the necessary paperwork, eager to be at Jerry's side.

"May I see my husband?" I asked the admitting clerk.

I did not know what had happened in the ambulance. I was calmly told I had to wait and directed to a waiting room at the end of a winding, twisting corridor.

All was very quiet at that hour. As I walked the hallway alone, I passed the female officer who had been in my home just an hour before. She was standing in front of a curtained area.

"May I see my husband?" I asked her.

She shook her head. "They're working on him right now. You can wait at the end of the hall."

I continued down the deserted hall to the "holding room", waiting to speak to a doctor. I had no suspicion at first as I pulled my knitting out of my bag and began working on a blanket for my grandson that I was going to continue on the plane ride to China.

As the minutes ticked by and no one came in to speak to me, I started to wonder what was going on. Anxiety crept over me as I sat, alone, with no idea what was happening and wondering why no one was coming to take me to see my husband. It started to feel like an eternity and I wasn't surprised when I "dropped" some stitches just like Madame Defarge in *A Tale of Two Cities,* foreshadowing for me what I began feeling in my gut.

This is not a good omen.

After awhile, a young female resident hesitantly entered the room. I shoved my knitting back in my bag and stood up, eager to follow her to Jerry. And then I looked at her…and I knew.

"He's dead, isn't he?"

The resident stared at me for a few seconds, totally dumbfounded at my confronting her on what I had started to believe was the reality of the situation. She had not expected that.

After a moment, she gathered herself and reluctantly looked

me in the eyes.

"Yes… I'm sorry."

I didn't say anything. I didn't know what <u>to</u> say. A feeling of calm washed over me. Perhaps I went into shock with the culmination of decades of knowing that that which I had always somewhat anticipated as a possibility had now happened. Based on Jerry's medical history, on some level I had always expected this moment – and now here it was. Jerry was dead.

Through a haze of shock, I heard the resident say that they worked to bring Jerry back for 45 minutes even though he had died in the ambulance.

"Would you like to call any family?" she asked gently, pointing to a phone.

I nodded, not quite able to absorb the enormity of this news.

"Would you like me to stay with you?" she offered.

I looked up at her and slowly shook my head. "No… I'll be fine. Thank you."

I knew it would be indescribably hard…and also knew I just had to do it. I remained standing as, one by one, I called each of my three sons. I started with Craig, our oldest, and my heart was racing as I listened to the phone ring.

"Hello?"

"Craig? It's Mom - Dad died."

My heart lurched as I heard him scream.

"Where are you??? What happened???" he asked in a voice deep with emotion. I heard and felt his pain coming through the phone as he took in the news.

Repeating those words, "Dad died", with my other two sons, first Gary and then David, felt as though my heart was physically breaking. Each of the boys reacted in their own unique way and I was grateful that each had his wife by his side as they wailed and cried. The sounds of their anguish and grief pummeled me to the core of my being. There was nothing I could do for them but listen. Their despair crushed my heart. There would be moments in the years to come when the sound of their screams would come back to haunt me.

Craig quickly began to make arrangements for his family to travel up from Florida as soon as possible. Both Gary in Connecticut and David in Westchester offered to leave immediately to be at my side.

"It's not necessary," I reassured each of them. "I'll be okay. Stay with your family." They were comforted by my suggestion of having our dear friends Phoebe and Ed meet me at home. Nevertheless, David and Tara arranged for a neighbor to stay with their sleeping girls and did drive the 40 minutes to be with us for a few hours until it was time for me to get a few hours sleep.

Craig, a cardiologist who knew that this was likely to happen at some point, said, "I dreaded this day." Despite his medical knowledge of this possibility, it was a shock for him as well for his two brothers – a shock for us all.

I wanted to see my husband one last time, which the doctor had offered for me to do after I called my family. I gathered my things and found a hospital worker to take me to him.

"Is someone coming to bring you home?" she asked.

I told her that friends were meeting me at my house and I would be okay to drive myself. She then led me to a fairly large room where Jerry lay.

He was lying on a gurney, his body covered with a sheet. A male nurse was sitting a distance away from him. I was grateful that his body hadn't been left alone. I knew this was one of the many Jewish customs pertaining to death and it felt right. In needing to say goodbye, I walked up to Jerry's left side and took his hand, a natural gesture between the two of us. He was still warm and his eyes were closed.

I gazed at him, this man that I love so deeply, with whom I shared three sons, six grandchildren, a home, a life, and my heart. I looked into his face, took a breath, and said, "I love you."

Aloud to the nurse, the room, and the universe, I honored our incredible half-a-century of laughter, adventure, honesty, family and deep soul connection.

"I had a great ride with this man."

I then turned back to Jerry, feeling for the last time his fingers touching mine, thanking him for his love of 50 incredible years, and kissed him goodbye.

On my drive to the hospital, I anticipated having Jerry next to me on the eventual ride home. Now as I walked out of the Emergency Room, I was struck with the reality that this was the start of a life without him physically by my side.

One journey was over. Another was just beginning.

SHIVA

September 3, 2005

Dear Jerry,

Shabbat Shalom! It's almost 1 a.m. and I can't sleep so why fight it. I will do what you did (I almost wrote "do") but instead of reading as you usually did when you couldn't sleep I'm going to start, that is, continue, writing to you. In the past, writing letters was always such a meaningful way of communicating for us and even though you died just four days ago I am planning to write letters to you. Marriage Encounter, the weekend experience in which we participated in 1974, taught us the skill of writing love letters to each other, which were based on feelings. Continuing that practice through the years both within a formal monthly meeting with other couples, and informally on our own validated the importance and benefit of communicating feelings. Thank you Jerry for agreeing to go on that initial weekend even though you suggested we take our tennis racquets so in case we were bored we would have something to do. I remember the racquets never left the trunk of our car during those 48 hours.

Of course this all doesn't seem real, as I feel so peaceful and comfortable in our bed, our bedroom, our home. I even felt that way at Temple Sinai (the venue for your funeral service), our "second home", as Craig called it. I am not sure why but not concerned with why. I'm grateful for those feelings right now.

As I'm writing I hear the murmuring of Craig and Gary talking downstairs. Or is it laughing? Or is it crying? Others have gone to sleep. Prior to writing to you I was filled with awe. Awe in having observed our friends and daughters-in-law planning, organizing, serving, straightening up throughout these first days of Shiva – awe in hearing the words of love, respect and gratefulness for you by hundreds of people – awe in experiencing two perfect weather days; days that would have been ideal for you and I to play golf or tennis, sail, bike, or relax at the beach or on our porch.

Instead, we are sitting Shiva for you. Even though I truly believe you can see all, I know that writing it down will help me process this transition. I will forever keep the memory of tonight in my mind.

Consecrating Shabbat, we all stood around the table with Josh and Matthew lighting two sets of Shabbat candles, David pouring the "wine" for all the little ones with the eight branched wine server I brought back from my last trip to Israel, adults drinking wine from our beautiful shiny sterling silver Kiddush cups that have been used by earlier generations, chanting the

Kiddush and Motzei and then pulling pieces from the challah as we have always loved to do.

We, your loving family, after sharing blessings and food, went to Temple to attend Shabbat services which were held outdoors under a blue sky and setting sun. Sitting there surrounded by my six adult children and six grandchildren, the youngest four climbing on my lap periodically, gave me a sense of well being and wholeness even though we were all there that night because you had just died. If not for that significant fact it probably would have been you and I sitting there that night as we so often did. When Craig told me he saw a feather floating down during the service I knew you were with us. As you used to say, "It doesn't get better than this."

The previous days have been filled with people arriving in our home to offer their condolences and receiving telephone calls from far away places like Chile, Seattle, Florida and Israel, each recalling times shared with you and how much you were loved and respected.

How special it was to see Craig with Johnny, Al and Mehran hugging, talking and reminiscing about their memories of studying in our home when they were in medical school. What wonderful memories of another purpose for our home, a study center for four future doctors.

I spent early morning time with Josh, our oldest grandchild, who recalled his week spent with you in July. It was just the two of you. (What a forever memory for him – a true final gift from you.) He said everything in the house reminded him of his grandpa. He then shared the letter he wrote to you before flying up from Florida for the funeral. I am filled with amazement by the depth of his feelings, beliefs, thinking and writing. His hope for you "to be at my Bar Mitzvah, holidays, and everything else in the future in your spirits" [sic] is everyone's hope. He also referred to you as one of his role models adding, "I want to be just like you." Craig referred to his letter during his eulogy but I hope to share its complete contents with others some day.

The pride I feel extends to our boys (well they really are men) and their ability to express their feelings openly and articulately, not only in their eulogies but with their friends and ours, with their wives and with each other's wives, with their children and each other's children, with each other and with me. I'll continue tomorrow.

Good night. I love you, Harriet

September 4 (1:00 a.m. again)

Dear Jerry,

I was planning to go to sleep around 10:30 but got to talking with Craig and Amy about a possible future family trip to Israel in honor of Josh's up coming Bar Mitzvah as well as how I was going to manage the finances, especially the job of paying bills which was your domain. Two sons have offered their help but I want to be as independent as possible and plan to use the services of the professionals we have connected with. I know I want to learn to pay bills by computer, something you resisted.

Earlier today "the boys", Josh and I went to early morning Shabbat services held in the Temple library. Both the small size of the room and the windows open to the trees and bushes made it a perfect place and time for reflection, prayers, triggers, tears and support.

Today our neighbor MaryJo was married. I went next door to see her being photographed outdoors in her wedding gown. Knowing I would not be attending the wedding as you and I had planned, she told me that your name would be included in the church ceremony. I was overjoyed. What thoughtfulness!

It's interesting that by following Jewish custom of not sitting Shiva during the Sabbath we all had time to be…to pray in Temple together, to rest, to be with just the immediate family. I liked that.

The highlight today was sharing some of the latest Marriage Encounter letters you had written to me. Craig and Amy, Gary and Shelley, David and Tara, our two oldest grandsons, Josh and Matthew and your sister Sue were all gathered on our porch. I believed it was meaningful for them to hear your most recent positive feelings about your life directly from you in the form of these letters. Immediately after reading those few letters, as the sun was setting, Gary led us in Havdalah. We had Matthew as the youngest person hold the braided candle. As we sang the traditional "Eliyahu HaNavi" and "Shavuah Tov" we held hands. It was as special as when Sally and Michael used to lead this service in the past. Of course I laugh silently when I think of you always joking about the "half dollar", your play on words with "Havdalah" whenever we participated in a Havdalah service.

I'm tired, so I will say goodnight now.

I love you, Harriet

September 4 (11:45 p.m.)

WOW!!!! Today was another perfect day for golf or sailing or tennis or biking. Can I also say it was a perfect day for Shiva? This house was filled with people of all ages and all sizes with all different connections to you. Some shed tears, some shared memories but almost everyone had nothing but praise for the wonderful person you were. I loved listening to others sharing their feelings or memories of you. And I talked and talked (twelve hours straight) about what happened to you on Tuesday, August 30. I retold the history of how after a quiet dinner for two on our porch you complained of not feeling well and all that followed in the next couple of hours until your death. I shared about our wonderful and magical weekend with four of our closest friends, Phoebe, Ed, Louise and David up in the Berkshires, the visit with Gary and Shelley and the grandchildren on the ride home, the normalcy of Monday and Tuesday, with work and exercise. I spoke of my gratefulness for what we had together and the fact that you did not suffer for a long time. I followed my need to talk and talk. That's what has always worked best for me when I am stressed. By doing so I take some control of an uncontrollable situation. I know we don't have control over death and we don't have control over grief. However, in all my counseling, I have always encouraged mourners to talk and write, talk and write, talk and write, for as long as they feel the need. Thanks for listening.

Good night. I love you, Harriet

September 6 (1 a.m.)

Dear Jerry,

As he left the house tonight, David hinted that I get a good night's sleep. Is this role reversal? I appreciate it for now. I intended to do that but I began talking with Craig about so many things like finances, his pending lawsuit at work, my work, and plans for future living. You taught your sons well about caring for their mother. Thank you.

Through friends we had learned that a moment of silence was held for you prior to the start of the annual Labor Day Weekend golf tournament at North Shore Country Club. I also learned that the flag flew at half-mast at Harbour Ridge Yacht and Country Club, our Florida vacation home community, in your memory. Boy, you will be missed; not just by me but also by so, so many people! You are missed already. Josh ended his letter to you saying, "Nanny loves you and misses you too."

I felt so sad when saying goodbye to Amy, Josh and Matthew as they had to return to Florida so the children can attend school and to Shelley, Allie and Grant who were going to fly to St. Louis to visit with her parents as part of a scheduled visit that they had postponed. Goodbyes are hard now for me. The reality is we never know if it will be a last goodbye to that person.

With my consent Craig has taken your watch, Josh your pocket watch (even though you never used it), three pajama bottoms, and Matthew, your blood tester.

I went to sleep for a little bit and then was wide eyed by 3 a.m. so I am continuing to write. This time I don't think it was caffeine as I was only drinking peppermint tea. I'm lying here staring and just realized I'm the first of my current friends to become a widow. My single female friends were either divorced or never married, with the exception of my childhood friend Ruth who has not been in my life for years.

So now, I'm about to start a different journey. As you know Marcia became a widow recently. Well we are already connected. It seems she came by the house the day after you died bringing some plastic ware to be used for the Shiva. I said to her then, "Well I guess we will be seeing more of each other now". Although we have had different experiences (her husband's death coming after a protracted illness and yours so suddenly) she is a peer, bright, youthful, has a positive attitude, likes to talk about her experiences and feelings and I believe we can be mutually supportive of one another. I find it ironic that you attended her husband Gene's funeral just five weeks ago while I had to work that day.

As long as I am up and writing I need to tell you about your funeral. With Rabbi White's consent I chose to have the service in Temple Sinai, our "second home". This was the setting for so many of our life cycle events; Bar Mitzvahs, confirmations, graduations, wedding blessings, and babies being named. Why not for a funeral? It was a fitting place for a "mensch", a beautiful human being, a man of your stature and your greatness. We were at the Temple by 9 a.m. and for one hour the immediate family received visitors in the Temple library. I had so many grown men weep on my shoulder as they approached me and shared in a few succinct words what you meant to them. "Best friend," "mentor," "a good guy." What a tribute to you. I always knew how special you were and I always knew how fortunate I was to have you as my husband for all these years. I didn't fully realize how everyone else you met and knew felt you were special too. I understand that by 9:15 there were two lines formed, one to sign the register and the other to see us in the library. Prior to going into the sanctuary, Rabbi performed the practice of keriah, the cutting of the ribbon, and led us in the prayer acknowledging God as the true judge even at this moment of disbelief. It was a harsh sound to my ears, symbolizing you being cut out of my life. I do know that all the Jewish rituals pertaining to dying and death are in order for the mourners to face the reality of this traumatic experience. Well it definitely did that for me. Strange that I had taught that when I was a Jewish educator and later in my hospice work whether with individuals or in groups. Now I am living it.

When I was led into the sanctuary with our immediate family I saw a sea of people, standing in the pews, reminding me of attending High Holy Day services, but this time rarely recognizing a familiar face. Each face blended into another. There were so many and I was shocked not only by your death but by the turnout of hundreds. You died late Tuesday night. This was early Thursday morning and people came from all over the country. As I took my seat in the front pew I was confronted with the nearness of your coffin. I chose a traditional plain pine box and on the top the Star of David. Our sons agreed that the choice was a good one, as you too, were uncomplicated with no pretense.

I hope you don't mind that I chose the traditional shroud for you in lieu of street clothes. I remember telling you that's what I wanted when I was to be buried. Judaism teaches us that we are born into this world with no earthly possessions and we leave the same way. That choice was also helpful for me in acknowledging the reality of your death. You will not need a business suit or golf clothes where you are going.

Your close male friends spoke. The rabbi spoke. Their sharing was great but your boys, our boys, now grown men, blew everyone away with their beautifully articulated and emotional eulogies. There was a thread running throughout, with repeated phrases of honesty, good listening skills, caring, good work ethics, a loving husband, father, grandfather, brother and friend. I focused on every word uttered. I did not cry. I was grateful I was able to be in the moment.

I am going to try to get some sleep, as it is 5 a.m.

I love you, Harriet

September 7 (7:30 a.m.)

Dear Jerry,

Today was the day we were to leave for China, a distant and exciting destination. I know how anxious you used to get when traveling alone or even sometimes with me by your side. I remember sitting by your side in a therapist's office as we learned that your travel anxiety was symbolic of a fear of dying and how you chose to work on those issues with her, a trusted and brilliant psychologist. Yet, recently you traveled twice by yourself to Los Angeles, once for a memorial for a respected colleague and the other for the 100th anniversary of an important client company. Dr. Israeli called me today and shared her belief that with your death you had overcome your fear of dying as you have made the "ultimate journey to an uncharted destination". And you did it alone! In addition, you made the journey with the dignity and grace characteristic of whom you were.

My body aches to touch you, to feel your loving hands once again. I used to tell you we must have been together in another lifetime as we felt so connected and so comfortable with each other. (Now I hope you really know we will never be apart spiritually.) I think that is why I feel peaceful in our bed, our home and right now in my heart. How fortunate was I to have you in my life for 50 years! 45 married and 5 getting ready for the "best ride" ever.

Yesterday, the last full day of Shiva, was so rich with emotion, sharing memories, observations and opinions of who you were. There was a flow of people who knew you well, along with those who only heard of you through one of the family members. There were those whom I have supported personally or professionally through the years. They came to give back to me that very same support with hugs, heartfelt words, and their presence. It was a "good Shiva." The purpose of the Shiva week is to give the mourners many opportunities to consciously grieve by remembering and expressing feelings and emotions. As the professional I have listened to many Jewish mourners who had found the Shiva to be a negative experience because people talked about sporting events, vacations or the weather with one another barely acknowledging the sole purpose of their being there was to comfort the mourner. This Shiva was a celebration of your life as was the funeral. My colleague Mike pointedly said, "How could this gentle, small man affect so many people in such a profound and meaningful way?" I ask the same question.

I had gotten a heads up about you from your mother, oh so many years ago – and she was correct – the "sweetest, most wonderful boy" became the sweetest, most wonderful man, always willing to grow emotionally and spiritually and how you did love – you loved me, you loved the boys and the women they married, you loved the six "jewels in your crown," as Gary said in his eulogy, your grandchildren Josh, Matthew, Jessie, Allie, Riley and Grant, your sister Sue, your friends, your employees, your competitors (well maybe I am going too far).

Yesterday was the start of the transition back to life as family and friends returned to their homes and their daily lives. Craig flew back to Florida, Gary to Denmark. Tara stayed all day with the girls, returning home late leaving David to stay for the night along with my dear friend and mentor, Cathy, who flew from Seattle to be with me for a few days. Then Gary returned from his business trip to spend Shabbat with me. How perfect is that!

No accidents, I say. I think you are helping from afar. This also happened when I was on the receiving line before the funeral service. Names of your business friends, who were always hard for me to remember, as I only met them annually, were flying out of my mouth just in time to receive each one. I know you were at my side prompting me. Then again, you were always at my side protecting me.

And that, too, is what you did when you took your ultimate journey. For the record, I believe you "died" in front of me when you became unresponsive lying in our bed as you chose to get ready for sleep. Even though you had complained of not feeling well the last few hours you were quite sure a little rest is all you needed. I did insist on calling 911 when you began sweating and after doing so your eyes closed, your body became still and I hope you heard me repeat, "I love you, I love you Jerry. You were the best," over and over again.

Then miraculously you began to move, opened your eyes briefly and the words "I...love...you..." formed on your lips as a final gift to me. At the time the police arrived you were "waking". When asked by the policeman what happened you responded, "I must have fallen asleep". You were known for your dry sense of humor. That was no sleep. Even though you left the house smiling and joking with the emergency fire department personnel you officially died in the ambulance enroute to the hospital. That was another example of how you protected me, for I was following in my own car. We call this the "wisdom of the dying". The last control the patient sometimes has is choosing who will and who will not be by his side at the moment of death. Yet you prepared me when you became unresponsive the first time. I have no regrets about that last evening together, or not being in the ambulance or about our whole life. It was "a great ride" and I thank you over and over again.

I love you, Harriet

September 7 (10:15 p.m.)

Dear Jerry,

This was a well-scripted day as the week of Shiva ended. It seems as though everything happened as though preplanned. David and I took the symbolic "walk around the block". (It is a ritual to help the mourner get back to life and for the soul to go on its own.) However, that is a bit hard in this village, as it is not laid out like a grid so we meandered down Bengeyfield, took a left on High Street heading south, crossed Hillside Avenue and soon found ourselves near the firehouse. David suggested we stop and acknowledge the help they gave in response to my 911phone call the night you died. We did. We then crossed back walking near the tennis courts, where David and you had played father/son matches. We noted two landmarks gone (the East Williston Florist and the East Williston train station's famous cupola), symbolic of life's changes.

You made your mark in life and I know how special you were in my life. Our children, grandchildren, family and friends stated their beliefs but what a legacy you also left in your industry. I have received hundreds of faxes and e-mails from around the world. One read, "We felt like we lost someone from our extended family." Others said, "All of us will miss him as an elder statesman in the Cashew business", "In all the years I've known Jerry, I've never known anyone to have anything negative to say about him, competitor or not," "Even though he was one of my competitors I truly admired him", "To me his advice mattered, his feelings mattered, his presence mattered", "It is rare for a man to possess the outstanding qualities so obvious in Jerry", "I can honestly say I am a better person for having known him", "There are no men in our industry who have the class and professionalism of Jerry Vogel".

You certainly were a giant (even though you had to shorten your pajama bottoms). You left a good name, an ideal in our Jewish culture.

I also spent quality time with family and close friends in person and on the phone. Not only did Louise and David return from Massachusetts with their hugs, love and support but Louise brought packages of home cooked food to feed not only our stomachs but the emptiness in our guts. She shared that she cooked nonstop after the funeral. It is something she loves and of which she can be in control. Cooking for her was a positive coping mechanism.

Lee and Jim joined us too for leftovers and a last visit before traveling to Europe. One conversation revolved around David's idea of creating a Zen garden in lieu of replacing the deck you and I had been planning. Lee said she has the perfect contact for such a project. Of course Phoebe and Ed joined us at after work and dinnertime was filled with talk, tales and tears. Louise and Dave had intended to return home that night but he agreed to stay, as we were all exhausted from our grief and the late hour. I have just finished up with phone calls with Craig and David and I am really ready for sleep. The power nap I had earlier will not make up for all the lost sleep this week.

I love you, Harriet

September 10 (2 a.m.)

Dear Jerry,

The only reason it's been a few days since I last wrote is because I've been spending much time with friends and family. The compassion and support has been amazing. Let me go back to Thursday. Shiva was over and I prepared breakfast for Cathy, Louise and David with freshly made oatmeal (comfort food). After fixing a light switch in the garage David and Louise took off. Cathy and I had the whole morning to be together. Not only has she been a professional mentor in the area of death and dying, she is a true friend and knows how to listen without judgment or advice.

How easy it is for me to let the phone answering machine work for me as I spend precious time with dear friends. (That was never easy for you.) The mail too is piling up and it's ok. It is sitting in a cardboard box, a practice started since your death by others who were helping me stay organized. Don't worry; I will get to it in a few days.

I got into my car to drive for the first time since my return ride from the hospital the night you died. It felt strange but normal I guess for that first of many "firsts". Meeting people in stores and on the street has forced me to acknowledge your death and it has been ok. Intellectually I know this is what I need to do to help face the reality; that is to tell the story over and over. Alice came by and shared that she and Bill might be taking Marcia out for dinner if Marcia was up to it and Cathy and I said that's the restaurant we'd be going to tonight. The bigger surprise was when we had arrived at the restaurant and having seen the three of them seated we walked over to say hello. We were all blown away by the "chance meeting" of two nurses, Cathy and Marcia who hadn't seen each other in years. They had known each other from another life working in the same hospital. WOW!!!

I knew that I needed to sleep in the house alone that night so Cathy went to be with her brother and sister in law. No writing that night but I did call Gila to wish her a happy birthday and called George to thank him for arranging Cathy's flight before she even had word of your death as she had been away at a seminar. I still can't believe I slept from 11-7, waking only to check the time on your clock by your side of the bed. Sleep each night is different. That is ok too. It's normal for a grieving person. That's what I have always told my clients.

Friday morning was what I needed; a leisurely morning to do household chores, laundry, put things away from Shiva, throw out food, repot a plant, and order my new butterfly (to replace the one that was recently broken). You bought that glass butterfly for me. Butterflies symbolize change and I need to have that symbol visible to me as I navigate this new journey.

After several phone visits from loving family and friends I decided to take a bike ride. Without planning, I found myself taking your daily route. You would have loved the smooth, newly paved road that was just completed in Old Westbury. Two ideas came to me during that ride. One, I will be more committed to publishing the workshop I created, "Coping With The High Holy Days After the Death of a Loved One" and dedicate it to your memory.

Two, I will pursue taking belly dancing lessons. Could that be a connection to the night you danced with a belly dancer on stage in Istanbul and had hundreds laughing and cheering you on as you were able to keep up with her movements, all due to your flexibility gained through years of yoga practice? That night will be a cherished memory for me.

Gary returned from Denmark and we had precious time together. We discovered that you had already taken care of the estimated taxes for September 15. What didn't you take care of? From bringing in the dry cleaning to doing dishes, from balancing my checkbook to mailing all letters and packages. I could go on and on. Your love was evident from the twinkle in your eye, the gentle way you spoke, to all the many things you did daily to make my life easier.

Sue, Gary and I went to Phoebe and Ed's for Shabbat dinner prior to going to services. It was the perfect place to celebrate Shabbat after Shiva. It was the venue for so many of our Shabbat and holiday meals since 1974.

Writing at 2 a.m. when I can't sleep seems productive and yet I know being productive is not the only important thing for me. I need to feel the pain and yet I know I can't force it. This morning I had a good cry as I was drawn to your side of the bed and saw the basket of books you kept as well as your handwritten notes on yellow legal paper about areas of growth that you had been working on. I cried for the courage of your openness to confront real issues and feelings and to grow and overcome them. And did you ever! You continue to amaze me even in death.

Did I tell you about the doves? After you died mourning doves came to our property and mainly were on the porch roof during Shiva. I learned they mate for life and I believe we too are spiritually connected for eternity. There were three doves on our roof the morning after your funeral. Well yesterday when Cathy and I were sitting on the porch, one dove was quietly perched on your rope hammock facing in our direction. Today there was one dove when Gary and I were outside talking. It seems like you're there with us. Whether that is true or not you did make your mark in your lifetime.

I love you, Harriet

September 10 (11 p.m.)

Dear Jerry,

Today was a trip down memory lane. Invited to join David and Tara at her mom's upstate country house, I drove north on Route 17 recalling times and places we had been together, starting with a fraternity boat ride up the Hudson River to Bear Mountain when we were teens, to weekend visits to hotels and bungalow colonies in the Catskills with family and friends and business colleagues. Dinner at Shelly and Mark's home was delicious. Dessert was apple pie a la mode. You would have chosen to have your favorite pie with the ice cream too, I know. But respectful of your diabetes you would only have had a taste. I talked, I laughed and I cried. And no one stopped me from expressing what I was feeling. That made it a safe place.

I love you, Harriet

September 11 (11:50 p.m.)

Dear Jerry,

I'm glad I accepted the invitation to travel upstate. I spent quality time walking and talking with David, sat with Riley as she had asked me to join her at her small picnic table to eat our lunch, and loved that Jessie, when waving goodbye, said to me, "Come back again Nanny".

I came home from my weekend to 21 messages, each one filled with concern for me at this time. I only returned two, one to Craig who said I could call up until 10:30 and to Yael in Alaska knowing it was hours earlier and she had already left several messages for me.

We would have been in China with our friends Judy and Kenneth if you hadn't died. They chose not to go ahead without us. Instead, on my return from upstate, I drove straight to their Manhattan apartment and we spent four hours together talking and I learned that they were hoping to have spent more time in Florida this winter with "Harriet and Jerry" now that they were planning to become snowbirds. It will be difficult for so many people to adjust to just my name. Everyone reminds me that it was always "Harriet and Jerry" or "Nanny and Grandpa."

I have to say good night as I'm tired after driving more than 300 miles over two days. I'm also tired because I'm grieving. It's hard work.

I love you, Harriet

PS The songs I listened to while driving were oldies and nostalgic and brought you closer to me. Of course I don't remember the titles but I am grateful I had that station on, a catalyst for memories and tears.

September 13 (10:30 p.m.)

Dear Jerry,

Having just come back from dinner with George and Barbara, I reread the letter he had sent me after your death describing how he felt about you. He began it by saying that he had been at his company for 40 years. "During that time I've been in contact with many employees and associates. I want you to know none of them can measure up to Jerry...As an owner of a company I could not have had a better man run my business than Jerry."

I was so proud when I read that. I don't want you to get a swelled head (joke, joke), as you never did. You almost always took things in stride. It was an amazing tribute to you in all ways. George even told me how he plans to continue paying me your salary this year and the timetable for your profit sharing that would be due you.

Josh and I had a heartwarming phone conversation whereby he told me about his rabbi's sermon Friday night relating to butterflies, their significance and he's writing in a journal Amy bought for him (with a butterfly on it). Wow! Some growth....

Phoebe shared a wonderful story too. She and Ed went to a store called Golden Oldies looking to buy three light fixtures.

When she was told she could bring them home to see how they would look she asked for some boxes to carry them.

"No boxes," replied the woman.

Then Phoebe spotted one and when she got closer discovered the name on it was "Vogel Popcorn". I googled the name and found out it was a ConAgra product. We are wondering if you knew of the company when you worked for ConAgra. By the way they produce 52% of popcorn in the US.

I played golf today with Helene and hit rather well including chipping in hole 6 for a birdie. Everything you taught me! Thanks for introducing me to the game of golf, for all the rounds we enjoyed together or with the boys or friends, near or far away, and for the gifts of golf clubs and lessons through the years. What a game! It's such a metaphor for life. It teaches us about what we can and cannot control. It teaches us that we never know where the "next shot" will go. It teaches us to learn from each and every experience. It teaches us to live in the moment. What a life sharing it with you!

I love you, Harriet

September 17

Dear Jerry,

Today is Craig's birthday, but of course since you don't have earthly concerns now you don't have to be reminded anymore.

How ironic that the card I already had for him was from a mother rather than from both parents. I'm sure it will be painful for him not to receive your handwritten personal message as he always did. So in your inimitable way please send him a gentle loving message and embrace. I'm hoping this photo (my all time favorite of you and your three sons) will fill him with the memory of your loving smile and other wonderful memories of his dad and brothers together.

Today I really am going to complete opening the mail that has accumulated since your death. I did a big chunk Thursday with Louise's help. I need to do this so I can begin the online bill paying process with Gary's guidance.

I hope you are at peace. I love you, Harriet

September 24

Dear Jerry,

One week later and I have so much to tell you. My intentions of writing daily have gone by the wayside. My days have been filled with people and paperwork. I finally finished opening the mail that had piled up since your death and I'm moving along with the bill paying process, thanks to Gary for setting up the program on the computer. It's really pretty cool doing it this way.

Socially, I am only accepting to go out with one person or one couple at a time. My reason is to have intimate conversations and have each share how your death has affected them. However, it seems like I'm out every night. That will change, I know.

Last weekend I went to the Berkshires to stay with Louise and David. I had offered to bring salad and my famous dressing for Alice and Bill's grandchild's birthday celebration over the weekend. Thinking I was in control, I had bought the ingredients, had everything washed, prepared, bagged and waiting in the refrigerator to put in the car for the next morning. It wasn't until I was about 45 minutes from home that I realized salad for 20 was still sitting where I had left it the night before, in the refrigerator. Not unusual for a grieving mind! I resolved the dilemma by going to a farm stand with Louise after I arrived and prepared another salad and another batch of "Harriet's" green dressing.

I am doing many things to keep my mind and body in balance – yoga, golf, biking and eating healthy. However, I felt great pain and tension in my neck the other morning. No wonder! Grief can do that. I quickly made an appointment for a shiatsu massage with Lorie – after that I felt remarkably better.

Tuesday I conducted two separate workshops called, "Coping with the High Holy Days After the Death of a Loved One," one in the afternoon and the other in the evening at the hospice office. They had been postponed from the original date because of your death. While my colleagues were concerned about whether I could or should facilitate these particular workshops I felt confident I could do a professional job and felt an obligation to host what had become an annual hospice program. Even though I was in acute grief myself I was gratified I could help others. I knew that by helping them acknowledge their fears and concerns, to think ahead, talk with family members and plan ahead, the bereaved would get through this holiday season with less fear and anxiety. That is what we have been doing too, to get through our upcoming holidays without you. The boys and I are talking and planning.

Can you believe that Mushroom, who became "your" cat, now stays in the living room since your death rather than in the den where she used to sit with you for hours? Is that her expression of grief?

Our butterfly bush attracted the most beautiful orange butterfly last week – I just knew it was a sign from you, just as the birds were during the week of Shiva when mourning doves walked on our roof constantly. I must also mention that the day after your funeral when Josh and I were in the backyard talking, he noted three birds on the roof and reminded me that Uncle David referred to Bob Marley's song, "Three Little Birds" in his eulogy. The message is "don't worry 'bout a thing, 'cause every little thing's gonna be all right". That's my hope and belief. I know the path will be sad but in the end it will be all right. Last night while Sue and I were having dinner on the porch we heard gentle sounds and sure enough there was one bird on the roof. Just checking in, were you? Is there a connection of all the birds visiting with the name Vogel, which in German means bird? Or is it a connection with the feather that drifted down from the sky during that Friday night service after your death? Will you send more feathers? I wonder!

Last week Sue and I had Shabbat dinner at Joan and Steve's home. Several people had invited us and I had originally accepted Phoebe and Ed's invitation inasmuch as theirs was the first call. However, because of an emergency they cancelled and I simply picked up the phone to ask Joan and Steve if their invitation was still good. Was it ever! We had a delicious meal and true support. No judgment, no advice, they just listened to us and we talked about you. Then off we all went to Temple.

And to think I am only writing about the highlights.

I love you, Harriet

September 26

Dear Jerry,

Today is our grandson, Josh's 12th birthday. He has been so amazing since your death, calling me, leaving messages and carrying on adult conversations. He is showing such concern for me and what I'm doing and how I'm handling your death. He shared with me a dream he had of you coming to him to inquire what happened. This is what he wrote in his journal. "September 15, Morning now. 7:05… Last night I had a dream, such a real dream. I was in New York and the doorbell rang. This was after everything happened. I opened the door, and it was Grandpa, my Grandpa. I was first crying, but then laughing in such happiness-like it wasn't possible. Then I yelled to everyone, 'Grandpa's here, alive'. Everyone screamed with joy. Then everyone hugged Grandpa, especially Nanny. I kept hugging him, like it was forever. Everyone got (their) own private time to talk with him. I told him what happened in the past two weeks, and asked him how he was sitting there right in front of me. He said he didn't know. Then he went to see Nanny. A few minutes later, I walked into the family room and Nanny and Grandpa were kissing forever. Then the dream was over, and I didn't get to say goodbye, once again."

It has been told that when someone dies suddenly it's a shock to that person's soul as well. The soul too has to adjust to the reality.

I am looking forward to Josh's return to New York this weekend so he can retell his dream to me in person.

I also plan to tell him as well as Craig and Amy that I cannot follow your practice of choosing stocks as birthday gifts for the grandchildren so I will send money to their accounts and their parents will have to assume that responsibility now.

I love you, Harriet

September 27

Dear Jerry,

Yesterday I began seeing my private clients in my home office and so far it's okay as I have been working with them over time. However, I have taken a leave from the hospice agency until November 21 and that's great. I didn't think it would have been wise to work with the newly bereaved. I need time to do what I have to do; grieve.

Tonight we had our Marriage Encounter meeting but we followed a different format. (Usually the meeting begins with a themed presentation by one couple and then each person writes to his spouse responding to a question related to the presentation.) Tonight each person wrote his feelings about your death and shared with the whole group. All the sharing was about you. Sad and grateful were my feelings; grateful for you in my life and sad missing you now and in the future, but it was agreed you would always be with us – so Jerry put down the date for our next meeting on your calendar.

I just reread the letter I wrote to you in 1975, the one you had saved in your top drawer – not too different from the one I wrote a few weeks ago at the last meeting we both attended. How special was our love! We knew it and never took it for granted. It was so different hearing about it from others though. Your effect on people was remarkable in how you cared for them and loved them in your gentle, steady and protective way. I feel so grateful that I was the one you chose to share your life with.

Today I met Judy in New York to view an art exhibit at my alma mater, Hebrew Union College. In the lobby when meeting a professor from my graduate school days, he made mention of my black ribbon. That brought me to share my story along with my tears. But sad is not bad. Isn't that the purpose of wearing the cut ribbon so others will acknowledge the reality of a recent death? I'm planning to wear it for the first month.

It turned out to be a nostalgic and healing visit for me as I recalled your unconditional support, financially, physically and emotionally, that paved the way for me to get my Masters' Degree in the 80's from that school. Thank you for that gift. It led to two careers, one as a principal of religious schools and afterwards working as an educator and a bereavement counselor in hospice. It is a gift that keeps on giving.

I love you, Harriet

September 28

Dear Jerry,

Tonight George, Barbara, Enid and I celebrated Ed's 70th birthday. However, the focus of the conversation was about you and your influence in the industry. George agreed to my request to attend the next business convention in January to say my good-byes to people and to a lifestyle I had shared with you. I know that too is something I need to do.

Everyday more letters, cards, and donations made in your memory are coming in. And everyday, I am taking care of at least one new item; phone calls, bank visits, and letters to make changes of status. I'm trying to fill your shoes with all the financial items as well. Because of your fine organizational skills it will not be hard to continue what you always did. The real challenge will be balancing the checkbooks. Hopefully with Gary's help and the computer program, I will master it.

I went to Winthrop University Hospital this morning to bring a basket of goodies and my thanks to the Emergency Room staff and doctor for trying to revive you on August 30. It was very, very sad for me to remember that night and I cried all the way back to my car in the parking lot. Yet I knew I had to do this. I think it helped me face the reality of your sudden death.

I love you, Harriet

September 29

Dear Jerry,

Lunch with Marge today was what it always is – deep, open sharing; nothing superficial. She said that you and I were the couple they could most identify with relative to our values, our "coupleness", our childrearing and our relationships with family and friends even though as couples we didn't see each other frequently. She regretted that this summer slipped away without our making a date.

I can't believe it's four weeks since I had my hair colored and cut on that day before your funeral, the day my two dear friends Phoebe and Louise and I were the only clients at the hair salon. That was strange enough. There was the usual "wallpaper music" on in the background. I'm thinking now of how I cried when I heard love songs that spoke to me of you but how we all laughed when we decided if someone were filming this scene at the beauty parlor it would have been called, "Three Hairdos and a Funeral."

Into the city to meet Phoebe and Ed for dinner and a show, a tradition we four had been sharing for years. We missed you, especially that we were eating in the same restaurant, Zen Palate, and were going to go to the same theater as we had done about four times a year. From our table, I looked out at Union Square Park, where you and I had walked on several occasions since 9/11. Remember how we decided it was important to go into Manhattan to visit some of the firehouses, get close to Ground Zero and walk through Union Square Park with all the signs and posters asking for help in "finding" missing people? It helped us face the reality of that horrific event as well as lend support to those firemen who lost their buddies. Going back to that same restaurant and the same theater helps me face the reality of your death as well and what we had and what I will never have again with you.

I love you, Harriet

September 30

Dear Jerry,

One month today. Jerry, it seems like yesterday that you died. My memory is so clear of the sequence of events from dinner through the final hours of your life, and yet sometimes it seems like months ago, as there have been so many people, activities, cards, letters, and conversations since then. Today is the last day for wearing my black ribbon. I found it important for others to see it and to say something to me, helping me retell the story. I wore it everyday including today through my professional and personal activities. When getting ready to meet Marcia, my newly acquired friend whose husband died five weeks before you, I looked in the mirror and the ribbon wasn't there. How timely I thought, no accidents! Marcia and I have so much in common. We will be seeing each other again for sure.

Craig, Amy, Josh and Matthew arrived from Florida today to be here for Rosh Hashanah, the Jewish New Year.

I love you, Harriet

October 1

Dear Jerry,

6:50 a.m. is a time that is meaningful again and again. That's the same time I called Louise and Dave on August 31 to tell them you died. It's the time I often awaken. I don't understand the significance yet but perhaps one day I will. I love you, miss you, wish you were here to see and enjoy the grandsons – they have grown light years since your death – sensitive, loving and bright eyed.

Josh and I played golf today and we arrived as the men were

finishing their round of a shotgun tournament. It was so sad for me thinking you weren't with them. I know you would have been if you were alive. Nevertheless, we had a wonderful time as we hit the ball beautifully, and when we had a bad hole Josh joked, "Grandpa must have gone to the bathroom." He knew you were there not only watching, but helping. Since the morning tournament was called "Greens Keeper's Revenge" the pins were placed in the most impossible positions for today and it provided Josh and I with many laughs as we attempted, most times unsuccessfully, to get the ball into the hole. It felt good to laugh.

I took the family to dinner at the club for "fine dining" as you would say. They dressed up and we "invited you" to join us. I missed you but knew this is what you would have suggested we do. It felt right and the truth is wherever I go people speak about you and that fills me with love and gratitude and peace.

I love you, Harriet

October 2

Dear Jerry,

You were missed throughout today as the whole family set this day aside to be together and celebrate Josh's 12th birthday. It was a perfect day to go apple picking and all thirteen of us knew you were there too when a single butterfly appeared as we entered the orchard. Yet it was very painful too. I took a photo of our sons standing together and they looked so sad to me, not just their faces but their body language too. Back at David and Tara's house we sang "Happy Birthday" to Josh and I presented our gift to him, as planned, the tallit and matching kippah I had purchased on my last trip to Israel to be used for his Bar Mitzvah next year. You can just imagine the tears it brought as we all faced the reality that you wouldn't be at his Bar Mitzvah or take the planned family trip to Israel next summer. I have recently learned that when Craig and Amy first shared with Josh the plan to go to Israel to celebrate his becoming a Bar Mitzvah, his response was to fly from Florida to New York to "pick up Nanny and Grandpa."

"Man plans and God laughs" is a commonly quoted Jewish aphorism…. and true once again.

I love you, Harriet

HIGH HOLY DAYS

October 4

Dear Jerry,

It's the first day of Rosh Hashanah 5766 and you're not with us. I remember the Rosh Hashanah when I agreed to drive with you to your home to see your parents. Up until that year I would not drive or write or work on that holiday. However, I was influenced by the fact that I liked your parents as they liked me and it seemed to be the right thing to do. They were to be my future in laws. I still recall looking out the passenger side window thinking God would strike me down for driving on a High Holy Day as I had been following a traditional Conservative upbringing. Well God didn't and my spiritual connection only grew and grew as did my relationship with your parents whom I lovingly called Mom and Dad. Since you were brought up in the Reform tradition I used to say we had a "mixed marriage". We learned from each other and created from that "mixed marriage" a family unit strong in ritual and tradition, a role model for family and friends. We established a home that others have always enjoyed coming to, to celebrate holidays and lifecycle events.

Last night was no different, with many people seated at our extra long table extending into the living room, except that you were not present leaving me to sit alone at the head of the table. But we spoke your names: Jerry, Dad, and Grandpa. We cried our tears; our hearts broke with the sadness of missing you, but we carried on in new ways. Craig, Amy and the boys led us in lighting the candles. How difficult it was for me to say the Shecheyanu, the prayer that acknowledges our gratefulness for staying alive to reach this season but I did sing it, although haltingly, choking back tears, for I am grateful for so much and for being here today. Gary, Shelley and the children led us in Kiddush over wine and David, Tara and the girls followed with Motzei over two round raisin challahs (your favorite). I then gave each grandchild a framed photo taken of each with you. When the tears subsided we were able to enjoy the dinner and conversation. That was possible only because we openly spoke of your absence and shed our tears first. I know it was a healing experience. It is okay to feel sad.

Temple was also painful for each of us as we felt the grief at different times and in different ways—different prayers and different songs triggered each of us. Our ritual kept us going. I even chanted the Torah blessings from the bimah, an honor given to me every year but this year my heart was heavy with pain as I haltingly chanted the words. So many triggers! So much sadness!

I love you, Harriet

October 5

Dear Jerry,

An alarm woke me (I set two) to be ready for a 5:30 am pick-up to go to Kennedy Airport for my trip to Nevis with Gary and Shelley, the children and Shelley's parents, Jay and Jill. Flying didn't seem so strange as I have traveled alone before without you. However, on the long flight there was ample time to recall our many trips together, especially to the Caribbean Islands and it made me sad knowing I will never travel with you again.

Going down to the beach felt nostalgic. When Gary and I talked we cried together as we both felt the pain of losing you, each in our own unique way. He shared how you taught him so much and how we enjoyed so many wonderful vacations as a family.

Allie turned to me while we were driving from the airport in our rental van and said, "Grandpa didn't want to die, did he?"

I didn't answer then but she saw my tears, my sadness and said, "It's ok Nanny."

How can a 3½ year old be so wise? I reassured her you didn't want to die and the doctors at the hospital tried to help you but couldn't fix your heart, the same words I used when she asked me on the morning of the funeral why you died. I hope I was telling her the truth. I know that is very important when supporting children who are grieving as long as you explain it appropriate to their age level. She held my hand while we were talking like she was my protector—and she was for that moment.

Dinner out just with the adults was really great—delicious food, fine wine, conversations, and a nice distraction from my sadness. It would have been so natural and perfect if you were here—the tree frogs croaking, the stars glistening, the balmy breeze blowing, and reggae music by the beach band—memories of times shared with you throughout our many trips to the Caribbean and British Virgin Islands.

I love you, Harriet

October 11 (6 a.m.)

Dear Jerry,

I'm up early today anticipating my return home—It was a healing week—a massage, golf, the water and much love and attention from Gary and Shelley and their amazing children. "I love you Nanny" goes a long way.

When I made a G in the sand for Grant, I also said, " G is for Grandpa".

I do know it is important for me to bring your name up in conversation with family, friends or even strangers. This will keep your memory alive. You will always be remembered in our hearts, thoughts, prayers and your name will be on our lips. I was amazed I could read for pleasure and enjoy listening to music and dancing with the kids—I think of how much we loved to dance.

While it's so easy to talk and cry with the children I felt pleased to hear from Craig and Amy independently that they are returning to a semi-normal life with sports, school, work and preparing for Yom Kippur.

I love you and miss you. Harriet

October 13 (6 a.m.)

Dear Jerry,

I can't sleep now so it must mean I need to communicate with you. I would love it better if I could roll over and touch you, hug you or feel your arms around me.

I arrived home from my week away ready to prepare for Yom Kippur. As family and friends gathered around to light the yahrzeit memorial candles, it was so hard to add a sixth one for you. Standing during the "Kol Nidre" prayer I found myself recalling having stood next to my parents when I was a child and thinking how our grandsons were doing the same in Florida tonight. The rabbi's sermon reflected that exact possible memory and the choir sang "L'Dor V Dor"—"from generation to generation". We did it! You and I continued our parents' and grandparents' legacy, created some new ritual and now I can proudly say our children and grandchildren will carry on for us.

Thank you, Jerry, for being by my side as we prayed, hosted holiday dinners and set the example for family and friends. Now this community we helped create surrounds me as I walk this journey. It's living Judaism at its best—and last night as I cried at the end of services, it was David who held me as I have held him at other moments. I am not alone but I miss you. (I guess this is the first time in 40 years that you fasted.)

I had found it strange that I hadn't received the usual gift of holiday nuts and candies from one of your customers. I was just about to call Phoebe to see if she had any nuts in her house that I could have for Break Fast tomorrow night when the door bell rang and there was a UPS delivery of two boxes of freshly roasted cashews from your company as though you had just hand delivered them. Thank you for this as well as the "tons" of nuts you hand delivered and shared with family and friends for every occasion through the years.

I love you, Harriet

October 14 (8 a.m.)

Dear Jerry,

I slept about ten hours exhausted from an emotional 24 hours.

During Yizkor I sat between Gary and David and we cried and cried and cried. The haunting melodies, the words acknowledging the fragility of life and the rabbi's sermon that seemed to speak directly to us about your life being taken from us physically but affirming you are and will always be with us evoked stifled sobbing and unabashed tears of sadness. Dear friends surrounding me, crying and missing you. Shelley and Tara stayed back at the house during Yizkor with their children when they wanted to be with us in Temple. I am not fully clear as to why we hadn't looked at our options like hiring a babysitter. I regret this happened but I know I have to let go of thinking it was my responsibility. Because our minds are not fully focused we had not communicated beforehand about this little piece. We talked afterward and cleared the air and this will not happen next year. I am grateful for that. I do know Amy was by Craig's side in their temple and for that support he was grateful. Break Fast was here as usual with family and friends and after all the crying and fasting we ate, drank and talked while the young children ran all around. For the moment we didn't feel sad. We felt whole. We felt hopeful as the New Year was beginning.

I love you, Harriet

October 15 (6:50 a.m.)

Dear Jerry,

6:50 a.m. again…it seems that no matter the time I go to sleep

I get up at this time. Many times I wake up with a "start". It's almost like I have to revisit the shock of your sudden death. I know that's the time I had called Louise and Dave to share the sad news that you died. Are you my new alarm clock?

Well, yesterday was eventful! First, constant heavy rain brought torrents of water into the basement—lots of towels went down. I rung them out and replaced them often but when I heard "plop, plop" I followed the sound to the oil burner room, saw water on the floor, noticing it was coming from two open pipes jutting out of the wall—buckets to the rescue, called the plumber and while he closed off these pipes, I learned they were old leads from the outdoor oil tank we abandoned. I didn't panic. I'll bet you are proud of me.

The second eventful experience was the show we had bought tickets for by phone when we were all together in the Berkshires. It was supposed to be the six of us, Phoebe and Ed, Louise and Dave, you and I. I chose to see it with them anyhow, and we made a reservation at a restaurant prior to the show. Of course, we made it for five, but when we were seated at the table it was set for six. We all agreed to leave it as was and I made a toast to "sweet memories and hope for the future." The show, "In My Life" was incredibly symbolic—our story in so many sub themes about life and death. There was pathos and humor and I laughed and cried. Again it seems as though everything has been scripted since you died. One song's title was "Life Changes On A Dime." While it was painful to listen to the words of the songs, likewise it was healing. Thankfully, I was surrounded by grieving friends; people you have touched deeply and who loved you. I felt protected when sitting right between these two couples, thinking of how you had always been my protection and you continue to be. For that I am grateful. You have always been and will always be a gift from God.

I love you, Harriet

Sunday, October 16

Dear Jerry,

The sun came out yesterday finally but today it's windy and in the 50's, a good morning for snuggling and making love but instead I'm writing you. Afterwards, I'll change over my clothes closet for a new season. I'm proud to say that yesterday I spent the whole day by myself doing errands, paperwork, making decisions and phone calls. I always knew you took a big load from me and I let you know how grateful I was for that division of labor but I'm handling it all and hopefully will be able to continue without feeling overwhelmed. After a productive day I ate a delicious dinner of leftovers alone and it was ok.

October 19

Dear Jerry,

Today was a meeting with lawyers dealing with change of wills and trusts. I also made an appointment to take care of Social Security changes.

I had hoped to donate your special new shoes to the VA hospital, the ones you bought reluctantly to help your feet that had been affected by your diabetes, but learned I couldn't because they don't accept worn shoes. And to think they are like brand new and I know there's a veteran who would love to benefit from them. I'll try another avenue but not sure what.

I saw a hematologist as per the advice from my internist. It seemed strange going to this specialist but my blood pressure of 110/70 told me I was "ok" with it for now.

Had dinner with Lee and Jim and sat at our favorite table at our favorite Japanese restaurant. Lee noticed I sat in your seat, so she sat in mine. I guess neither one was willing to face the empty seat. They are so sad and each told me separately about the many issues they are dealing with since their daughter's sudden and untimely death just a month before yours. Our plans are to meet in December at the same restaurant in Huntington that the four of us were planning to go to for your and Jim's birthdays. Happy it won't be but meet we must!

I find them so courageous to be with me in my grief as they experience their own for Kathleen and you.

I love you, Harriet

October 20

Dear Jerry,

Lying in bed this morning I thought about my first trip (hope-fully, if the newest hurricane doesn't take the intended path across Florida this weekend) to our vacation home without you. Sadness overtook me thinking you wouldn't be with me when I enter Craig and Amy's home as we had often stopped there directly from the airport. But I know deep in my heart you will always be with me, with us—we are too connected by love that has lasted lifetimes and will hopefully continue that way.

Last night I experienced a new feeling after attending a surprise birthday party in Manhattan. I left early and while walking to my car said out loud to myself, "What a waste of time and en-ergy." I felt so lonely. I felt alone in a group of people, some of whom I knew. Surrounded by "strangers". I recognized I had little patience for party talk. Perhaps it was not the time to go to a party. Or perhaps I expected others to acknowledge what I was going through. It made me feel even more grateful for the loving relationships we had cultivated; the warm loving parties and get-togethers and the continued unconditional love and support from our closest friends.

Yesterday I went for my annual appointment with "our" der-matologist. The news of your death was received with shock and sadness. The doctor, when reminded about your long his-tory with diabetes said, "Life would only have gotten worse," which I knew.

This really was a tough year for you with the foot ulcer, trigger fingers, leg pains (poor circulation?), less stamina which you shared only the day before you died, and possibly other symptoms you weren't talking about or weren't fully aware of. You lived your life with courage, vigilance, always willing to learn and do something to help yourself live a fuller life and you did. You were a true inspiration. I love you for all that you were to me.

I love you, Harriet

October 21 (11:30 p.m.)

Dear Jerry,

Tonight Judy looked at your photo on my computer screensaver and said she thinks you are "just away". Am I thinking that too? Am I still in shock two months after? How was I able to host two couples for Shabbat dinner? "Easy," I say, "I've done it hundreds of times." But is it easy? Is it by rote?

We talked about you. I sat where you usually sit and where I sat on Rosh Hashanah too. No tears; just missed you. When I was cleaning up after they left I was thinking of how you would have helped me, then taken care of the bar and turned off the music. I did it all including calling the emergency sewer cleaner because I noticed a sink backup as the dishwasher was running. They will be here tomorrow morning at 8:30.

Bill and Alice will be leaving for their trip to China tomorrow. I wish we could have made our trip as planned but we did travel to so many wonderful places and I have a lifetime of memories of many vacations. How fortunate we were!

I'll be going to Froma and Mark's home in East Marion this weekend as you and I had planned before you died. I hope it will be ok for me.

I love you, Harriet

October 22

Dear Jerry,

I had a wonderful day with Froma and Mark—the drive out in the rain by myself, a delicious lunch of freshly caught grilled fish (by Mark) and Greek salad, heartfelt and teary sharing of feelings (isn't that what Marriage Encounter taught us?) —then joined by Phoebe and Ed—some local shopping including purchasing anniversary gifts for our children. They are museum quality, hand blown, rainbow colored vases that reminded me of our purchasing your favorite piece of art, the glass sailboat, in Murano, Italy. We ended the day with a lobster dinner at our favorite restaurant on the east end of Long Island. Yes, Jer, I would have shared the large pieces of lobster with you, but I don't think you would have had the patience to pop in and out of stores and wait while our friends made their purchases.

I love you, Harriet

October 24

Dear Jerry,

I was to have flown to Florida today to spend Simchat Torah and attend Yizkor services with the children. However, Hurricane Wilma slammed across Florida today and I'm holding a seat for tomorrow. I lit yahrzeit and holiday candles before going to Nina and Barry's for dinner of delicious brisket. But it would not have been good for you; too sweet. We talked deeply as usual and when I shared my feelings of gratefulness that you didn't have to live a debilitated life with increased side effects from your long-term insulin dependent diabetes, Barry said, "Jerry was kissed by God."

How sweet a phrase! I loved hearing it because no one deserved that kiss more.

I spent time today with Ina, as she asked me to come to her home, needing help to create a memorial for her late husband Bob. Being in that home brought back memories of times shared with them. We talked and cried as we swapped stories sitting on her overstuffed Victorian style sofas.

The hurricane did wreck havoc in Florida once again with 3 million without electricity. I have no idea yet if our condo and community suffered damage. I'm now rethinking purchasing the wind insurance you had been contemplating. (I found such papers in your desk.)

I had an exciting early morning meeting with the landscape

designer presenting her ideas for the new garden. I loved them and I'm hopeful it will bring new beauty and peaceful, positive energy to the backyard. I'm thankful for David's idea that instead of replacing our deck as we had planned with a new deck that I should consider creating a Zen garden instead. It should also bring the property value up. I am following your lead to keep the house up on all levels.

I am taking care of each new challenge as it arises, e.g. the flood, electrical fixtures needing rewiring, sewer backup, oil burner not igniting, and strange noises from the alarm panel. Are you sending me challenges, or signals that you are with me? I know you're always with me just as before, whether I'm thinking of you or not

I love you, Harriet

October 25 (6 a.m.)

Dear Jerry,

I was up at 5:30 a.m. to check the water in the basement (we've had a Northeaster all night) and checked on my flight to Florida. Cancelled! What a bummer! I tried to go back to sleep, in vain. I'm disappointed as I was looking forward to seeing everyone but on the other hand, the roads are probably filled with debris and traffic jams with no electricity available. I'll continue calling and checking on friends and family who live in Florida and perhaps this is the time to start writing acknowledgements to the hundreds who have made charitable donations in your memory. I will go to Yizkor services today at Temple Sinai and I'm confident David will be pleased to join me for that.

I love you, Harriet

October 26 (8:00 a.m.)

Dear Jerry,

Yes, I went to Yizkor services with David and I was grateful for the tears. What prompted them? Was it the music, the words, the venue or my missing you? Perhaps it was a bit of each. I spent the rest of the day at home alone sleeping, reading, writing, knitting and working on the computer. It felt peaceful.

I'm going to use the book *Mourning and Mitzvah* to help me get in touch with my feelings. I've recommended this workbook to others and have used it professionally. It's now my turn to write down answers to the many questions and prompts offered in this workbook. Here goes.

It's been two months since your death. You died on a Tuesday so maybe I need that quiet, contemplative day to be a Tuesday each week. I love writing to you and talking about you to friends and family. When I think of you I remember your sweetness and the ease of our relationship.

The last thing I remember you did was to say something funny to the emergency people relating to the oxygen mask they wanted to put on you. That memory warms me as I always remember you made me laugh and smile, ever since our teen-age years of dating. In fact I remember laughing when you were the brunt of a joke in the frat house the first night we met. As we and other couples were dancing the lights dimmed and one of the fraternity brothers claimed they had to turn off the lights "to save money to buy a tie for Jerry."

The biggest changes for me since your death are not having you to hold me when I sleep, and my handling the mail, bills and all household responsibility. While I was always grateful for your doing the latter, I knew I could do it if I had to. As for the former change, sometimes at night I hold myself and think of you.

During your life I told you in so many ways how much I loved you. I hope you also heard me when you became unresponsive on that fateful Tuesday night. I said over and over, "I love you, I love you, I love you. You're the best. You're the best." If you were alive I'd hug you one more time and repeat those same words.

I hadn't expected the sense of peace I feel in the house and outside, but then again I really didn't think of that before. The biggest surprise for me is the lack of daily tears. Oh I've had my share and sometimes I've been sobbing uncontrollably, for example when I'm in synagogue, when greeting and say-ing goodbye to family and certain very close friends, when I visited your grave by myself after the funeral, when hearing "Unchained Melody" on the car radio, when I saw the show, "In My Life" and when I watched the movie, "In Your Shoes".

The hardest thing for me up to now was calling the boys from the hospital after midnight and telling them you had died and listening to their reactions, the shock, the cries, the wails, the disbelief, the questions, the heartbreak in each child's body and all I could do was to just listen with a physical pain increasing exponentially in my own heart. I'm sure I was in shock. I don't believe I was stoic as that is not my style. I am a crier. You knew that. I even cry at TV commercials and when watching a Disney Broadway show. Perhaps it was simply because I always knew in my heart that one day this might be what I would face.

After hearing the many stories from the bereaved, and experiencing my mother's long-term dying from Alzheimer's disease and your mother's long and debilitating cancer, and being realistic about the worsening side effects of long-term diabetes, I believe your sudden death was a "kiss from God." And I'm grateful for that, firstly for you and secondly for me and thirdly for all who loved you. It's not that I wouldn't have cared for you and have done my best, for you always deserved that and got that, but you would have had to make so many adjustments, grieved so many losses. You already coped with that for 40 years. God bless your soul now.

I hope you are at peace. According to Jewish literature for the first three to seven days the soul is potentially confused as to whether it is alive or dead. I noticed that corresponds to the week of Shiva. It always amazes me how helpful the Jewish customs and laws relating to death and dying are for the bereaved today even though they were developed about two thousand years ago. Perhaps they also were intended to assist the soul on its journey after the physical death. I've also read that it's hard for the soul to find peace when the death is so sudden like yours, but I pray it will come quickly to you. The truth is, right now I have no fears for myself. I am awaiting blood results but I'll deal with it. I'm proud of how I'm handling this new part of my life. I'm grateful for the medical leave I have until November 21.

In losing you I have lost my best friend, your unconditional love and support. But as I shared during Shiva, I had so much from you for 50 years that I believe I have enough for the next 50. I remember after I said that to someone, I turned my head around as if to say, "Who said that? Who put those words in my mouth?"

Yet I wish you were here with me to help make decisions and to answer questions that repeat and repeat in my mind. Are you peaceful? Are you angry you left your physical body? Left me? Left us? Left your life here on earth? I know you struggled with the concept of dying and you worked hard with a professional about your anticipatory anxiety, which she believed was a symbol for fear of death and basically your not being in control. When I found the book, *The Next Place* by Warren Hanson in your book basket next to your side of the bed I opened it, reread it and sobbed, grateful that perhaps you saw "the light." The final pages of the book read, "I will cherish all the friendship I was fortunate to find, all the love and all the laughter in the place I leave behind. All these good things will go with me. They will make my spirit glow. And that light will shine forever in the next place that I go." You made your greatest and most challenging journey to "uncharted destinations" with the "grace and dignity" with which you lived your life. (These were the comforting words I received from your therapist.)

I hope you now know it's ok to die and that God will protect your soul as God protected you in life with loving family and friends and caring doctors. What I always needed to hear you say was "I love you" and you did that over and over again. I felt your love and now I know that everyone else did too. As my colleague Michael said during Shiva, "How can this little quiet man affect so many people?" You obviously touched them with your love, your sensitivity and sensibility, your courage and your work ethic. I could go on and on. What I would have liked to know is if you had a premonition about your death at age 68. I wish you could have understood and I think you did, that my hope in calling 911 was for your benefit. I may have regrets that I didn't call early enough but I have no anger that you kept saying you thought it is probably a stomach virus or indigestion, delaying my actual call. How well I remember that same scenario when you had your first heart attack 17 years ago. You told me you thought it was just a stomach virus. Yet since then we learned that nausea is one of the warning signs. I never wanted to make you an emotional invalid. I trusted your judgment and your way of caring for yourself for all these forty years living with diabetes. I remember early on when I consciously made the shift to not questioning you or telling you how to handle it. I may have given you a "look" and there were times I was frustrated and thought you could have better control to prevent some low blood sugar reactions, but I always said to myself, "Not until I am living with diabetes will I know how difficult it is for you." Just recently I had a "scare," a thought that I might be diabetic. I lost some weight (by consciously eating smaller amounts and healthier foods), drinking more (hot tea feels good and fills me), urinating more (because I'm drinking more). But, no, I got the call back from the doctor and there's no protein in my urine and blood tests were normal.

I am most grateful for the fact that you didn't suffer in your death or over a long period of time leading to death.

During the course of counseling the grief stricken I usually ask two questions; what do you miss the most and what do you miss the least? You and I used to joke about this and yet it is crucial to honor the humanness of the departed. It is easy to recognize some typical things people missed like the companionship, the humor, the intimacy and the security. Some people would say the least thing they missed was the illness, the arguing or the control of the TV remote control. What I don't miss about you are the food stains on shirts and ties, an "inherited trait" from your mom, and the blood stains from blood testing and insulin shots on your shirtsleeves. Isn't that amazing that that is it! How inconsequential! I'm glad we talked and joked about that as we had openly talked about so many important things as well. What I do miss about you is your sweet smile, your gentle and stable presence, your soft touch, your embrace, your open heart and ears. You were always willing to listen to me. I miss you in bed, and when exercising or washing up in the morning as we got ready for the day. I miss you on the golf course, you sitting at your desk in the corner of the den and driving together in the car. Yet it feels like you are near, never far away. I believe you're close to me, at least in my heart. I will emulate your courage with health issues I will face. The thing I will do differently is how I pay bills. You can't believe how easy it is to pay online. Yes, I regret that I didn't learn this before and share some of the responsibility. You could have had so many more free hours to watch TV, read or whatever. And yet that might have taken away your sense of self, as protector and caretaker. It was what was, and I am grateful for all you did for our family. Please protect and love them from above and I will do my best here to love and support them. I pray you are at peace under the "sheltering wings of God." I love you, I miss you and wish I had one more chance to say, "I love you," so I will now.

I love you, Harriet

Rereading what I just wrote has validated the need to revisit the life, illness and death as one travels the grief journey, just as I have encouraged my clients. I am so glad I did this exercise.

October 28

Dear Jerry,

I have been questioning my grief. Am I grieving too little? It is quite normal to question one's grief. Many clients have questioned the intensity of their grief. A typical question has been, "Why am I crying all the time?' Just to let you know I spent time with Rabbi White. He pointed out my particular situation, being both the griever and the professional. He helped me recognize why I've been conflicted at times. While I am instinctively the grief counselor, I'm not sure how to deal with my raw emotions and yet I am able to compartmentalize my life and able to function well daily, and to be clear and focused when working with clients. After the meeting with him I "found" (literally it popped out from a shelf at Barnes and Noble while searching for a book for Matthew) a book called *Grieving Mindfully* (a Buddhist approach) and it all makes sense. I need to observe my grief reactions, not try to analyze or question them and definitely not judge them. Isn't that what I've always encouraged my clients to do? I feel better about this. In the past weeks I had been looking for validation from my colleagues and some close friends. Now I will just be and observe, feel the feelings and let the grief take its necessary and unique course for me.

I love you and grieve for you. Harriet

October 31

Dear Jerry,

Last night I spent one hour on the phone with Kris (you would call it a "visit" since she lives in Michigan). It was important sharing and crying, reflecting about the funeral, the relationship, the memories and the fact that yesterday was two months since your death and the birth of their grandson Luke. She said she and David always remember the phone call, the shock and their drive rushing to the airport so they could be here for the early morning funeral. She told me how special it was for them to perform the Jewish custom of helping fill in your grave. As dear friends they performed a final act of love as you entered your "new home." That they learned from Rabbi's words at the cemetery. I remember learning that this mitzvah is ranked very high as one performs it without any possibility of being thanked in return.

The other day I was left a package in a manila envelope in the mailbox. In opening it, I found a note from Lee, "Dear Harriet, I wanted you to have something from Kathleen. With much love, Lee." Inside was a beautiful gold ring with a blue topaz stone. I cried thinking of this young woman, their daughter, who died so suddenly and so young. I cried as I took off my emerald ring, the one you bought for me on our trip to Brazil, and have been wearing this new gift for the last three days. I've cried every time I look at it or talk about it and now again as I share the story with you.

This weekend was the weekend we planned to have Jessie and Allie, the oldest girl cousins, for a sleepover and take them the next day to the NY Philharmonic Very Young Peoples Concert. I kept the plans for the three of us. When we went to Eddie's, our favorite family pizza restaurant, Allie referred to the fourth chair at the table and your not being there. Both were open in talking about you, your death and their sadness. I will always encourage that so they can remember and have you close to them. "Your seat" was then used for Allie's doll. The girls helped me plant 100 tulip bulbs so we can look forward to their growth and beauty in the spring.

Today I will have the housekeeper help me "close up" the porch, something we always did together. It is always a sad day for me as the summer season ends. I'm thinking now of our last dinner there the night you died and of your naps on the couch, of your reading in the large chair, the gathering of family or friends for breakfasts or dinners, our Marriage Encounter meetings and most recently the many combinations of people sitting there and talking with one another during Shiva. I must not forget that the furniture is the very same that filled my parent's porch when we were dating. So many memories attached to one little room.

I love you, Harriet

November 3

Dear Jerry,

I've been at David and Tara's since Monday night to care for the girls so they could get away for a much needed vacation. It has been easy because I'm just focusing on the girls. It's almost a mental vacation from my grief as I'm trying to be in the moment. Surprisingly, I am not thinking about you as much. But I am talking about you with the children whenever the occasion is ripe. They each have their photo of themselves with you on their night tables.

While the girls were in school I drove to visit Lauren and her new son, Lamine, as she lives close by. Of course she spoke of "Uncle Jerry" and was grateful we attended her wedding but wishing you could meet her baby.

Spoke with Craig one night and Gary the other as they were checking up on me as I babysat. Each shared their reactions to receiving the letter advising them of the probate and a copy of the will, acknowledging how you always took care of their needs and the family's. No one expected to receive any money. The surprising comment from each boy, but for which I am grateful, was thanks to me as well as you in knowing we had made this decision together. It is always so beautiful when actions are appreciated even if that is not the reason to do something.

I received a call tonight from Amy advising me of the dates for a Bar Mitzvah trip to Israel next July. I thought about being there without you and everyone else being coupled. I had a lonely feeling but I know when I'm there I will love it and live each moment to the fullest. I know you will be there too with me. Well, life goes on, doesn't it? It's such a gift. I'm thrilled Craig and Amy are continuing the Bar Mitzvah plans they started before you died and likewise, Gary and Shelley are once again exploring their plan to move. I'm hoping David and Tara will return home renewed, reenergized and ready to "pick up the pieces" of their lives.

I'm enjoying this balmy weather by playing golf with friends.

One notable comment has been our friends' childrens' reactions to your sudden traumatic death as pure shock. You were alive, working, playing, talking, laughing, and on a turn of a dime you died, one final breath and no more. It's so surreal sometimes and yet very real to me. You're not here in the house or in the car. You're not coming through the door, playing golf or planning to fly to Florida on Wednesday. In that sense it's very real. I just replaced some light bulbs in the kitchen and packed my golf clubs into the travel bag, cleared pine needles from the gutter; all things you would have done. Each activity acknowledges for me the reality of your death.

Thank you for always doing and teaching me, too.

I love you, Harriet

November 10 (10:30 p.m.)

Dear Jerry,

I'm sitting outside on the terrace in Florida looking at the lights across the river, listening to faint sounds of sprinklers and insects, feeling peaceful, the same word I used to describe the feeling when I first visited this community years ago.

Direct from the airport I visited Craig's new medical office and felt a painful joy. My heart raced and my stomach felt empty. You would have been so proud. I cried. I cried for both of us.

When driving to the condo I cried again thinking how you weren't here to enjoy this special place with me again. I have so many wonderful memories. Coming into the apartment was actually welcoming even though it was crowded with the stored outdoor furniture. After counting the blown out screens from Hurricane Wilma, I slowly and mindfully moved the furniture outside, set out the accessories, cleaned up dead bugs, prepared both bikes, took care of the golf cart, took a small bike ride and ended this enjoyable and beautiful day with dinner with Barbara and Charlie, such good friends, wondering if you and Maryann are together in heaven? Remember, it was they who introduced us to this wonderful community. I missed sharing this wonderful day with you. But I feel your nearness giving me strength to live my life as we always did.

I love you, Harriet

(Maryann died from cancer days after Jerry. I had just visited her the previous week knowing the probability that I wouldn't have that chance again after our return from China.)

November 17

Dear Jerry,

As you know there are two important questions I always ask when I facilitate the bereavement groups. "What do I miss the most? What do I miss the least?" I would advise the bereaved that their answers could change as they too change during the grief process. I often think about those two questions. I'm noting the changes in my answers.

For today, I miss your body next to mine, especially since it's getting colder. Sometimes I will turn over and extend my leg onto your side of the bed recalling how we would intertwine our legs. But you're not there and I only have the memories. Now I know why I was drawn to a display of soft cuddly socks that I purchased recently. The three pastel colors coordinate with my pajamas and I hope you can see them from where you are.

What don't I miss? It came to me after I had Josh and Matthew for a sleepover in Florida and took them to the annual Stuart Air Show, played golf with them and had a very physically active weekend. It was busy but easy, carefree. I came to realize that I didn't miss my concern for you at the same time that I was responsible for the grandchildren. I hadn't realized until this weekend how much time, energy and underlying "worry" and "concern" was part of my life as we lived with your diabetes. I thought of how many times you checked your blood sugar, made adjustments in your insulin, food or activities. Was it so low that you needed to sit down and rest or even abort our plans? Now I better understand why I feel lighter since you died. Now I understand why I'm not overeating, a sign of my being stressed. Now I understand why I can be focused. There is relief. There is freedom. And those are normal feelings as well.

As a partner for forty years in your healthcare it was so much a part of our life I never appreciated how much energy it took from our daily living. I guess what I'm really saying is I don't miss the diabetes and how it affected our lives. But I miss you and I would have you back in a second with all the responsibilities, concerns and fears. I did it for so long I know I could have continued to share the challenge as long as you needed me. You did it all so effortlessly, never complaining, with grace, courage and responsibility, that I never truly realized I too was part of that until last weekend. I miss you so!

I love you, Harriet

November 18

Dear Jerry,

I am so fortunate that I am sleeping well, 8-9 hours a night. I meet so many people who cannot sleep or have altered patterns when they are grieving. Even though last night I slept only six hours I awoke at that mystical time of 6:50 a.m. again.

Forgot to tell you Gary and Shelley went to contract on a new house.

I love you, Harriet

November 19

Dear Jerry,

Last night I went to the first "event" since you died, and was surprised that I handled it as well as I did. I drove upstate to the Temple (not easy to find in the dark) for the Shabbat/Bat

Mitzvah service and then to the reception at another location. I drove alone, walked in alone and was a single adult among many couples. I felt welcomed by many and loved hearing a few people speak of you and me and of our "coupleness". Even when I miss you I know you're not far away. I believe you helped me find my way last night. Since the party was so close to their home, I slept at Gary and Shelley's and got to see their future new home the next morning. It is on a beautiful property, a lovely country street, and they can move right in and live there while their dream house is being built.

In a letter I received from a business friend there were reflections of his relationship with you and his observations of us as "the perfect couple" and he asked didn't we feel that way too and were we appreciative of being together? Oh how often we did acknowledge that to each other. I have no doubt of that. We wrote the words. We spoke the words. We lived the words. And often!

I love you, Harriet

THANKSGIVING/CHANUKAH

November 23

Dear Jerry,

As I lay in bed this morning, the day before Thanksgiving, I try to anticipate tomorrow at your sister's home—it will be the first Thanksgiving without you. I think of the yearly Thanksgiving Day at your parents' home many years ago, and of the many times afterwards when you've carved the turkey for your sister Sue after her husband Danny died. I think of how it will be different. Yet last year was different too. All fourteen of us were together on a family vacation in the Turks and Cacaos celebrating so many milestones, not the least being our 45th anniversary, and I like to add the prior 5 years that we dated to total 50. I am so grateful that we had this time together. What a gift you gave everyone by taking us all away. What joy, what memories to last a lifetime!!!

The year before that, our Thanksgiving plans changed too

when our grandson Grant was born earlier than expected. And this year will be different as well.

My thoughts are now racing ahead to Passover and what that may be like without you. Ironically, we changed to a different Haggadah last year and it is as though we set a new precedent. I always comment how every year is different, whether it is the people around the table or the seating arrangements, the leaders or activities—but none can compare to your absence this coming year. You are missed; you will be missed.

I love you, Harriet

November 24

Dear Jerry,

Just to catch you up I returned to work at the hospice agency this week. I was ready physically and mentally. I spent a similar Tuesday to the day you died; worked all day, returned home for a client and then had a light healthy dinner, but I ate alone this time and thought of that last meal we shared. Last night I went to "your" Monday night yoga class and joined the regulars and imagined you doing your routine. I noticed it was ok, as it has been in going to restaurants we have enjoyed together in the past. I think it actually helps me to reflect on the times together and to confront the reality that it will never again be that way for you and me. I'm learning that sad is not bad.

I love you, Harriet

November 25

Dear Jerry,

Today is Grant's second birthday and I wish you could have been here to see his face, experience his passion, hear his well articulated speech, and tell him how proud you are that he went "poopie on the potty" as we all were yesterday at Thanksgiving dinner. You're missing so much. It's so sad that you're not with us as we are living life. But I must believe you see it from where you are. If that is true then you saw your sister's beautiful Thanksgiving table, her lovely new home, the delicious turkey and stuffing, her reaction when I brought a box of cashews, her words welcoming us and acknowledging the changes and sadness, my tears when she was speaking, my sharing memories at your parents' home, how she reached over and held my hand for support, how Allie stared at me empathically as I cried, the silly adults putting on birthday hats when singing "Happy Birthday" and Grant's joy in seeing the candles and eating his cupcake with a spoon.

There were calls from the other children acknowledging their missing you this Thanksgiving Day as this was "Dad's holiday" they said. They recalled you watching the Macy's Thanksgiving Day parade every year just like your father before you. So many of us did that this year to remember and feel close to you.

I am grateful for what I have now, my health, my awareness, my support system and what I had with you, and our family's unique Thanksgiving in 2004.

I love you, Harriet

November 28

Dear Jerry,

I had a beautiful weekend—This holiday weekend was filled with connecting with many young people, our children's peers, and each one acknowledging your death and what your life meant to each of them. Many who live far from New York said that when they heard about your death they wished they could have flown back to New York to reconnect with their friends they grew up with. Your effect on this generation, I learned, was very powerful, both your life and your death. And so many young people did fly in for your funeral, so many young people that you mentored formally and informally or hired for either a summer or a fulltime career position. I still marvel at your scope of influence.

How lucky I was to have been your true love.

I love you, Harriet

November 30

Dear Jerry,

Today is three months since your death. Where are you in your journey? Where am I in mine? I still feel peaceful and clear-headed and I assume you are still loving me and taking care of me. Last night was a perfect example as I was driving home from Manhattan in a torrential rainstorm. I detected a problem with one wheel, and guessing it was a flat I made a quick deci-sion to continue for the last four exits knowing I would ruin the tire, hopefully not the rim, as it would be safer than pulling off at that late hour and in those conditions. I wasn't even worried and I thank you for helping me with that decision.

A funny thing that has connected me to you is that during the last two Broadway shows I've seen, I've snoozed during part of each, something I used to chide you about and rarely did myself—it made me laugh.

I'm saving some money by changing the cable package as I rarely watch TV. Three months, am I still numb? Help me un-derstand myself.

I love you, Harriet

December 3

Dear Jerry,

I'm down in Florida again and having a busy time, with sports and family and friends. The weather is outrageously beautiful.

Amy has been working hard (selling her "stuff" before the holidays) and you would be so proud of her. I know she misses not being able to talk to you about her small business.

The highlight of the day was a call advising me that the board of your professional association decided to hold the annual golf tournament at the upcoming convention in memory of you, saying it was a true honor and a tribute to a wonderful guy. The caller couldn't see the tears in my eyes but could hear it in my voice. There has been a range of reactions from our children and friends, all thrilled with the news.

I love you, Harriet

December 8

Dear Jerry,

Sunday was a sad day for me from the moment I said goodbye to Craig after 18 holes of golf, through having dinner with David and Louise before flying back to New York. As beautiful as is the weather, as comfortable as I am in our condo, as safe as I feel with close family and friends, there is hole in my heart.

I miss you.

It's December and it's cold now with two brief snows already. Your birthday is coming up and Gary and David are planning to go to the cemetery with me.

I'm busy now writing acknowledgements and don't know how long that will take. Also doing end-of-the-year computations as you always did.

I'm shipping our outdoor furniture to Brian and Gila as I won't need it with the meditation garden to be created in the spring, They have moved into their new home in Florida. They were over the top with gratefulness to be having "something of Uncle Jerry's" in their home, a table Brian sat at many times he said, and as recently as at your Shiva.

I've had some new thoughts about the unveiling of your monument. I'm hoping to hold it when the family is up from Florida at Passover but Craig was hoping to have it later, connecting to a visit for Rosh Hashanah. We're talking and that's good. I have always counseled mourners to communicate with family members when planning rituals, holiday celebrations and any upcoming events. Everyone's needs have to be considered.

I spoke with my cousin Howard who just had the unveiling for his grandson Jacob's gravestone this past weekend. I felt so sad reliving the memories of his funeral, the throngs of people, his friends and classmates as honorary pallbearers, the police escort to the cemetery, and how painful to watch Helen, dying from pancreatic cancer herself, at her teenage grandson's funeral and burial. I remember how you secured a chair for her to sit graveside rather than stand on that bitter cold March day. I also remember how during our last dinner out with Howard and Helen before she died, how you got up from your chair, walked to her side to help her cut her food. My mind jumped to so many family and friends who have died, especially this past year. Five cousins alone! My tears are running down my cheeks as I miss each one but most especially you.

I love you, Harriet

December 13 (12:40 a.m.)

Dear Jerry,

What am I doing writing at this hour? Much is on my mind. For one we held an annual bereavement event at hospice called "Healing Stories". This is an opportunity for the participants from past bereavement groups to share their stories of healing from their significant losses after the last year or two. Naturally it is very emotional for those who attend but it reminds all of the hope for healing from grief. Some of the stories were inspiring and I felt proud that I have been a part of that process as the professional supporting them with hospice services and counseling.

I have been writing acknowledgements, paying bills, and planning to give photos to our children—of you and them, for Chanukah, just like I did for the grandchildren at Rosh Hashanah. Writing to you now has slowed down my body and mind and I will be able to go to sleep soon.

I love you, Harriet

December 13 (10:30 p.m.)

Dear Jerry,

Had dinner, as planned, with Lee and Jim in honor of both your birthdays and I gave Jim one of your watches as a reminder of the "watch story" that we have shared since our vacation together in St. Croix so many years ago. I love it whenever Jim retells the memory of you and he having had a few rum punches prior to entering a store where you saw a watch you wanted to buy. However, when you chose to show it to me, I in my pragmatic manner responded, "But you don't need a new watch". Of course you did buy that watch and several more in your lifetime. We laughed and cried tonight for both you and their daughter. Lots of sadness between us but there were smiles and gratefulness too. They gave me a banner that reads, "Shalom" (Peace). I told them I will hang it on my bedroom wall.

"Happy Birthday Dear Jerry"! Well I know you never liked rushing it, but it's almost midnight. I need some sleep to have strength for tomorrow.

I love you, Harriet

December 14

Dear Jerry,

This would have been your 69th birthday. We, Gary, David and

I, went to the cemetery to visit you in your "new home" (at least where your body lies). The ground was frozen with some snow remaining between the newly sprouted blades of grass.

David saw a double rainbow; "Just like at the beach in St. John's when I was on vacation with Tara," he said.

Our tears froze on our cheeks. We were bundled in hats, hoods and gloves. David was dressed like you in wide wale corduroys, a green cable knit sweater over a white turtleneck. Sad we stood, alone, and then together in different combinations… we three, saying Kaddish, huddled together against the cold and emptiness we felt—missing you—more and more each day. I said to myself, "You're not coming back." I will see you again only when I die."

I love you, Harriet

December 20

Dear Jerry,

I'm here in Cabos San Lucas with Gary, Shelley and the children, a trip you and I were supposed to have made together with them. The area is beautiful but hilly and spread out and I wonder how it would have been for you walking the hills and distances. Would you have had another foot ulcer if you had lived? Would you have had leg pain?

A really strong sign happened the first day we arrived. The

preordered food was waiting for us in the kitchen. Sitting on top of a counter was a loaf of bread wrapped in cellophane with the company name clearly in view. It read "VOGEL'S".

Last night held a sad and poignant moment for me as I watched Gary and Shelley dancing to a romantic song. I sat at the table and relived the many times I experienced that with you. Oh did we love to dance together.

Dancing after with Allie and Grant to a Mariachi band was fun and I felt very much alive but now I will go to sleep by myself in a luxurious queen size bed and miss you.

I love you, Harriet

December 25

Dear Jerry,

While flying from Mexico to Florida I felt somber, then sadder, as I began thinking about January 15 when the boys and I will be attending your business convention and the memorial golf tournament named for you. I began writing down some ideas of what I might say at the ceremony, releasing many, many tears. I ignored the fact that I was sitting next to strangers on the plane. I'm noticing that my sadness increases when I'm saying goodbye to loved ones. It happened again when I said goodbye to Gary and his family when we took different flights out of the Dallas airport. The parting reminds me of my physical separation from you.

Tonight I held the Chanukah party in Florida that you and I had planned before you died. The condo was filled with two and three generations of families, similar to each past year. It wasn't easy but I spoke about our tradition of this annual party and how you would have wanted us to continue it. As wonderful as it was, with the children playing dreydel and other games like potato sack races, eating latkes and jelly donuts, singing Chanukah songs, lighting candles and laughing, you were missed by everyone. Of course we spoke openly about you not being here and I hope that was healing for all of us. I know it was sad but again I continue to see that sad is not bad.

I spoke on the phone with a recent widow who happened to be a friend of a friend, listening to her story and sharing my coping experiences. This casual conversation was helpful to me as well. Yet, in the last week our son went to a funeral of a peer whose life ended tragically and our friend's mother is now hospice appropriate. There is so much sadness. That's why I'm convinced more than ever to keep a positive attitude and focus on gratefulness as I live each day fully. I'm thankful for my life and I'm thankful you were my partner for so many years.

I love you, Harriet

December 28

Dear Jerry,

At the Chanukah party I loved hearing our great-niece, Emanuelle, tell me, "Uncle Jerry can see and hear us. He's like

God, all around."

Her openness is so natural. I know she has clear and loving memories of you in her life.

And I was able to share calmly with a new acquaintance, "I'm recently widowed".

Twice yesterday I spoke about the upcoming memorial golf tournament and found it's always received with, "Wow," but accompanying it are usually tears.

In transferring boxes of your clothes from my car to Amy's car for donation I saw Craig visibly affected as he touched a pastel striped shirt I had kept separate in hopes he might want it. He did want it very much. You are wearing that shirt in some photos in their house he reminded me. I remember when you bought it. You loved that shirt, or was it I who loved that shirt? Anyway, I loved seeing you in it. I loved seeing you in so many shirts or sweaters. I loved seeing you.

For Chanukah I gave Craig, and will do the same on Sunday to the others in New York, a copy of Billy Crystal's *700 Sundays*. Gary borrowed from that theme in his eulogy when he said, "2028 Sundays wasn't enough time. Not when the time needs to be split between all the activities; golf, sailing, hockey, coaching, modeling, mentoring, fathering, grandfathering, and all the numerous things we did together."

In addition, I gave Craig the photo of you and the boys sitting in front of the piano. That was my all time favorite of the four of you. That's why I kept it on my desk at work. When I gave a framed photo of you and Amy to her, she said it was always her favorite one.

I love you, Harriet

December 29

Dear Jerry,

Interesting how going to a movie with a grandchild can trigger so much emotion and so many memories of our life together. In seeing the sequel to "Cheaper by the Dozen", I was brought back to memories of our parenting, and to our first time becoming grandparents, watching our children parenting, and our dancing together. The legacy is long and I feel fortunate to have danced so many dances with you.

I love you, Harriet

December 30

Dear Jerry,

Well I'm packed and ready to go back to New York following our original plan, one week in Mexico with Gary, Shelley and the children and one week in Florida in our condo. Tomorrow I will be able to celebrate the last day of Chanukah with our other children and grandchildren.

You would have loved these two weeks away doing all the fun things we always loved to do. When out to dinner with Jane and Gary and a few other friends, Gary said the sweetest thing, "I know of a great foursome in heaven" and he named the four, you being the latest of his and your golf buddies who have died. How true!

There are times I can't believe you're not here with us and yet I'm planning the unveiling of your monument. I just looked at the calendar—four months today. No wonder I needed the tiramisu for dessert! It's comfort food.

It always feels so comforting to be with some friends. I can say anything. I can be me! Not so with everyone. Why am I surprised?

I love you, Harriet

January 1, 2006

Dear Jerry,

Whew! A new year! What does it mean? It means plans. Planning for the unveiling of your monument and hosting Seder in April, the convention in Florida beginning January 12, Allie's birthday on January 14. Life goes on. The last two days attest to that. After arriving home on New Years Eve, I opened two weeks of mail, played with the cat, shopped for food and then had a special treat for dinner by myself, set the table and finished wrapping gifts for today's Chanukah party.

I made lots of latkes today and Gary said they were the best ever—but it was a bittersweet day. Sue joined us and the four grandchildren were precious, playing well together and enjoying their gifts. We were so sad though. I acknowledged we were sad but added, "Grandpa would want us to continue to celebrate and we can be happy and sad at the same time."

Miss you so!!! It was sadder here than in Florida because this home has been the setting for countless Chanukah celebrations as well as other holidays with family and friends through the years. Judaism teaches us to keep the holidays, even in our grief. It attests to the continuity of life and distracts us momentarily.

Gary told me he had a dream of you and as he spoke tears rolled down his cheeks. David too has dreamt of you. I guess you know who needs you. Keep up your good work as protector and caretaker.

After talking to all our children and your sister and their processing this reality, the date of the unveiling will be the week of our anniversary and the second day of Passover, a time of rebirth.

Remember when you recited from the Haggadah, "Come my fair one…" the time our family Seder was on national TV? Maybe I will read that poem from "Song of Songs" at the Seder this year.

I love you, Harriet

January 5

Dear Jerry,

This week had me connecting by phone or in person with many of your business friends and I often heard, "Not a day goes by that his name is not mentioned," "I couldn't make the call initially because it was so hard," and "I can't think of a convention without Jerry; without you as a couple."

Apparently, we created many memorable moments for a lot of people. It feels like we had just won an Academy Award. The big difference is that we weren't acting. You and I worked hard learning to communicate clearly and lovingly and living each moment each and every day.

Thanks for being my partner for over 45 years. Thanks for being the "handprint on my heart" (a song from "Wicked"). To think tickets for that show were to have been your birthday gift but instead I took Linda as her Christmas present.

You came into my life to love me, teach me and you have. I had always said we must have been predestined to be together—it was such a perfect fit. And once again I want you to know how grateful I am for every moment with you, every loving look, every soft caress, every time we held hands, every moment shared silently or talking, playing or watching sports or walking side by side, just knowing you were in my life and now you continue to be my strength and support whether near me or as far away as the distant stars.

I love you, Harriet

January 9 (7 a.m.)

Dear Jerry,

I've been spending hours over the last months rereading every card, letter, fax, e-mail and donation, and acknowledging each one individually. Rereading just reinforced the theme from before as to how special you were and fortunate I was to have been your life partner. I finally feel I'm close to the end.

I know how healing this activity has been. It acknowledges the reality that you have died. I have shared that concept professionally with my clients. If possible it is important for the widow or widower to write those thank you notes rather than pawn them off to a relative or friend.

Friday night I drove into the city to Phoebe and Ed's apartment. Louise and David met there too as they are in from Florida. We were hosted for Shabbat dinner preceded by a champagne toast to 'friendship' followed by a grand tour of this newly decorated second home. It is fabulous in all ways. I wish them years of good health to enjoy it together. How special that the three of us were their first official guests. You were missed. You belonged there with us, we said.

Now here's the latest news but somehow I know you already know. A "new baby" arrived here on Saturday, January 7. Pepper Ann is her name; given to me by Cara, her rescuer, who thought I would give her a loving home. She added that she thought this was a good time for me to have a new source of love and comfort. By the way she is a black and white kitten, adorable and sweet, and it feels "right" to add her to the family. I had always wanted company for Mushroom but you never did. Well now I can make that decision by myself and I did.

I love you, Harriet

January 11

Dear Jerry,

It looks like Pepper is here to stay. Last night I had both cats sleeping with me for the first time and Mushroom is hissing less, a sign she is adjusting.

My daily routine at waking since you died stays the same. I lie in bed, stare or think until I decide to either write or meditate. Now I have the extra attention from Pepper too. She is another source of healing.

The anticipation of attending the convention is building. Whenever I tell someone that the golf tournament is being named in your memory that person reacts with a surprised look or "wow, that's really special". I couldn't be prouder of you and what you meant to so many people. You had such a gentleness and sweetness and fairness about you – people felt comfortable around you and accepted by you too. What a gift! What a gift I received in God matching us up together.

The boys are booking their flights and hotel rooms. After the golf tournament they are planning to head up to our condo and stay and play golf there together.

I have no idea how I will react to all those familiar faces and the greetings I will receive and the comments but I will stay strong no matter how sad. Sad is not bad.

I love you, Harriet

January 12 (11:30 p.m.)

Dear Jerry,

Here I am, Jerry, at the Sheraton Bal Harbor, attending the convention we had both planned to attend. Flew down by myself, took a cab to the hotel, and checked in before having dinner with Ed and Enid. How many years had we followed the pattern of having dinner with them on the first night we arrived for the annual Peanut and Tree Nut Processors Association Convention? But this time you weren't with us. Today was their wedding anniversary as well, so I toasted them, something you would have done.

When I returned to my hotel room an arrangement of red tulips was waiting for me from my sister with a card acknowledging my courage. How thoughtful! I called her immediately as it was only 9 pm in New Mexico. You have really worked your magic once again as Susan and I had such a loving conversation.

Good night. There will be more to share as the weekend unfolds.

I love you, Harriet

January 13 (11 p.m.)

Dear Jerry,

I kept the annual day of golf with our Boston friends, Becky and Aram. Their friend Mike completed the foursome. While he played beautifully and it was fun to have him, he graciously said, "I can never take Jerry's place," but appreciated that he was included.

The condition of the golf course was ugly and poor. I told them you were laughing wherever you are as you always chose a fabulous course for our annual golf game but this time Mike had picked it.

Back at the hotel I encountered many regular attendees who came up to me and acknowledged you and your special qualities and how great it was that I came. It was so nostalgic for me as this convention had been an annual ritual for about 40 years.

At dinner there was more conversation focused around missing you. I loved hearing it all. Interesting how that doesn't make me feel sad. It fills me with your essence. We all miss you. You were the best!!!

I love you, Harriet

January 15 (12:30 a.m.)

Dear Jerry,

It was Allie's 4th birthday yesterday.

The wind is howling. It began last night. The temperature dropped and it's cold in southern Florida. For me it was a family day: a walk with Brian, a visit to his home, lunch with Craig and Amy and a visit too from Louise and David who drove down from Boca.

Spoke to more business friends at the cocktail reception. Everyone says the same thing, how much respect they had for Jerry Vogel and how much they miss you. One said, "Coming to the convention will never be the same. I will always think of him."

January 15 (8:45 a.m.)

Dear Jerry,

Today's the big day—the Jerry Vogel Memorial Golf Tournament. I am grateful I slept last night even though I could hear the ocean's roar as I lay in bed. Yesterday's strong winds have died down as well as changed direction; the skies are clear blue and the temperature is really cold—in the 40's. Hopefully it will get to the 60's. I am doing everything I know to stay calm as I anticipate being with our three sons, listening to more accolades for you and offering my prepared words before the golf tournament begins.

I meditated, showered, did yoga and am now writing. I love you more than I ever knew, perhaps more than I ever told you. I know I told you often both in writing and verbally. Your legacy lives on in so many ways and in so many people. The sound of your name resonates with love, kindness and integrity. Remember when I told you the only thing I would miss the least if you died will be the stain on your clothes? It's true. That's all! I miss so much. I love you. Be with me today as always.

I love you, Harriet

January 16 (7:30 a.m.)

Dear Jerry,

Thanks for being with us yesterday. There were so many surprises as well as anticipated moments; the trophy engraved, "Jerry Vogel Memorial Golf Tournament", gifts of golf bag watches, again with your name imprinted, and speeches honoring your life, professionally and personally. During the pre golf ceremony I shared my words of appreciation that the directors chose this venue to honor your memory and personally how attending this convention for over 40 years had become an annual highlight for you and me.

I ended with my thank you for, "...some amazing memories. Memories of special people, memories of lasting friendships, memories of beautiful hotels, memories of spectacular scenery, memories of fun tennis and golf tournaments, memories of dancing and singing away the hours and memories of planning for the following year. I wish all of you good health as you continue on your personal and professional journeys and I hope you help keep Jerry's legacy alive, work hard - play hard - make people your priority - and be grateful for every day you're given."

Simultaneously three blackbirds circled above us, a visible reminder that "every little thing gonna' be all right", from Bob Marley's song—and it was.

The boys and I had a wonderful time together after the initial anxiety and much needed tears. We started our scramble format on hole 18. Do you think that was symbolic too as it means life in Hebrew? Gary had a fabulous drive. David then placed his ball on the green and I putted in for a "birdie."

We were all elated with that start but when Craig wanted to know how he helped I answered, "You drove us to the golf course in your car." This round of golf was much more than "a walk spoiled."

"It was heaven on earth," said Gary. It was a great foursome. But you were missed.

And now the group—our sons, the three little birds—will be driving up to spend time together in our condo—something they have never done before. Each one made the effort to leave their families and work to help acknowledge this tribute to their dad and extend it one day to strengthen their bonds with each other. I can't think of anything "cooler" than that. I am crying as I write this and am grateful for the life and legacy that can never be taken away. Be peaceful! I am, but I continue to miss you more and more.

I love you, Harriet

January 16 (11:30 p.m.)

Dear Jerry,

I feel like a Hollywood star. So many people came up to me tonight to say how glad they were that I had come and invited me to return next year. I graciously declined that invitation as this is no longer my life and I know it. I came this time to say goodbye and to give others a chance to say their goodbyes to me (and you).

In front of a record attendance (over 400 people) you were remembered with your name on a huge screen and a moment of silence.

Having won closest to the pin I was awarded a prize, photos were taken and I recalled the past wins and good times we shared at these annual conventions for so many years.

While standing and talking to friends sharing how they always remember us dancing I heard the band playing 1950's music, the same music that we must have danced to hundreds of times. Not an accident I believe.

Today I led my last Monday morning women's special event. Fifteen of us went kayaking. The weather was beautiful and everyone had fun. Afterwards, "the group" took me to lunch. Remember when years ago I suggested an optional activity for a couple of women who did not attend the business meetings? Through the years the number of women increased and the activities changed yearly from hiking to horse back riding to hot air ballooning to canoeing and to kayaking. The women offered words of thanks, goodbyes and a beautiful gift. Wow again— not just for the memorial golf tournament but recognizing how we had made an amazing impression on the PTNPA members forever. Those conventions were such a rich part of my life. And I will miss them.

I love you, Harriet

January 17 (6:30 p.m.)

Dear Jerry,

My first dream of you - I awoke about fifteen minutes ago realizing I saw you. You didn't speak but it was you. We were walking for exercise, you to my left, and I noticed you were having a hard time.

I said to you, "You're pushing yourself, aren't you?"

You looked at me in a certain way acknowledging the truth but refused to stop. You tried to hide the nausea but then suddenly stopped walking and began to regurgitate. I instantly knew I

could sit and write to you all day long. There is always so much to tell you.

I love you, Harriet

January 27

Dear Jerry,

Shabbat Shalom! I went alone to services tonight. It was okay. I remembered the first time you and I went when the services were held in the Martin County Realtors Association Office. Then we continued when Temple Beit HaYam built the new building in Stuart. The most poignant moment for me was witnessing a couple near me with entwined hands the way we used to do. It reminded me of shared hours in Temple and how connected I felt to you and God. I only hope you feel the peace now as when we were together here on earth. Before the Kaddish they sang a song based on one of Hannah Senesh's poems. I loved it. The words are beautiful. "There are stars whose light reaches the earth only after they themselves have disintegrated. And there are individuals whose memory lights the world after they have passed from it. These lights shine in the darkest night and illumine for us the path." I may use it for the unveiling ceremony.

I love you, Harriet

January 30 (11 p.m.)

Dear Jerry,

Five months today—can one believe the amount of time that has passed? It's all so relative. I spoke to Bob Gardner tonight after several attempts on both our parts. His wife Alma died four years ago he told me. He seems to focus, like me, on the many fulfilling years they had together. He also shared as so many before him, of the special love he had for you, "a really great guy," he said. I plan to call him at least once a year to keep the connection that goes back decades.

Last night I came home to a very cold house but by the morning a serviceman was here and fixed the problem. Ironically, the outdoor temperature was 60 and I was able to drive home from the city with the top down. How strange is that? It's winter.

Pepper is walking all over me so since it's almost impossible to continue writing I think I'll turn the light out and go to sleep.

I love you, Harriet

February 1

Dear Jerry,

I just returned from the annual "surprise" birthday party for Alan. They had many photo albums of past parties and you were in all of them. In fact you and Gene (he died five weeks before you) were standing side by side at Jane and Alan's daughter's wedding. Marcia and I both loved seeing that as it was not a memory either of us had. Tonight, Marcia and I drove to the party together. I call that synchronicity!

Today was the last session of the bereavement group I have been facilitating for 9/11 surviving spouses and partners. Five long years from devastation and despair to coping and love and new beginnings and laughter—what growth! It has been very gratifying for me to accompany them on their journey. They inspire me in mine.

I love you, Harriet

February 3

Dear Jerry,

Had a colonoscopy this morning and told the doctor and his staff about your death so they could remove your name from their records. That too was a moment of reality. I missed you being my chauffeur as in the past but with planning all changes have been possible, I see. Phoebe drove me there and Linda picked me up.

I love you, Harriet

February 6

Dear Jerry,

There is always so much to share with you. I wish you were here to hug and to talk with but that is not my reality. I just can't. Pepper is at my side purring. She's a great comfort and something new to love. She's actually being accepted by Mushroom and has become a positive stimulus for her in her old age.

Nicolas, our French foreign exchange student when he and Craig were sixteen, now grown with children of his own, came to New York for business. We set up a date for lunch and once again I loved hearing his stories and memories of when he lived in our home so many years ago. He told me that his wife Helen and his parents had shared their shock and sadness as well. Nicolas spoke of so many instances such as dinner alone with you (he now does that with each of his sons), my 40th birthday party and the sheet cake that I shared with him as he turned 16, our Passover Seder and how we raised our boys. It was like you were right there with us at the table. After lunch I drove him downtown to find an outfit (costume) for his birthday party in March. It was a typical day in NYC with no parking spots to be had but one appeared miraculously and we both knew you had something to do with it.

Being with other friends this week had me questioning—will it always be like this? Talking about Jerry? I hope so, but I realize it will lessen as our family, friends and I continue to adjust to your being apart from us physically, and adding new people to our lives.

I went to Friday night services alone again. It was called a "Healing Service". There were no tears for me this time but rather an opportunity to sit quietly and experience the healing of music, liturgy and silence.

There is so much to do now; paperwork that is, but I'm doing it. You would be proud of me. There are bills, decisions, record keeping, preparing for taxes, meetings and phone calls with financial advisors and lawyers. I know that this all will lessen in time too. I'm really ok – you helped prepare me on so many levels. Thank you again for all we had together and for your love that continues to nurture and guide me. I am forever grateful to you and God.

I love you, Harriet

February 7 (12 noon)

Dear Jerry,

Driving home from the lawyer's office I heard "Never Will I Leave Thee" sung by Robert Goulet. I cried the whole way home thinking how sad it is that you're not here with me and I'm dealing with wills, estates, taxes, transfers, trusts, legal paper work and inefficiency by some. I still believe you are guiding me or at least I choose to believe that. John said it best this morning. He is spending hours working for my benefit with no reimbursement because of his love for you. He said, "It helps me stay connected." You continue to be by my side too.

I love you, Harriet

VALENTINE'S DAY

February 11 (9 a.m.)

Dear Jerry,

Down in Florida again just sitting quietly on the porch look-ing out at a serene scene. It's a perfect day with the sun out, the temperature is warming and the birds are tweeting and the wooden chimes are ringing. I feel your presence but I wish it could be like it was, you and me sitting here about to do some yoga on the rolled out blue rubber mats.

I got a call from Alice asking what I was planning for Valentine's Day, inviting me to join her and Bill for dinner as we had done as a couple in the past. I imagine my response might have been unexpected as I answered, "Thank you, but I will be working until 7:30 pm and then I am scheduled for a massage. That's what I need to do."

I do realize it will be a different Valentine's Day for them without us. But then again, it may not be quite as different for them as it will be for me. I am proud of myself for remembering to follow the very suggestions I have offered to the bereaved as a counselor. Plan ahead for significant days and express one's needs even if that seems to contradict what friends and family think you need.

Amy called too but with concern for my being able to fly back to NY Sunday as a blizzard is approaching. I am not going to panic. I will focus on seeing Lee and Jim today as planned and play some golf together.

Had a great few days with Louise and Phoebe who stayed here in the condo. Talking, massages, walking, biking and the unconditional love and support from these two friends is so healing.

I went to Temple again Friday night, this time with Mickey and Dinny. This was the third week in a row and it feels good for me to sing, pray and be still. It is healing even if it is sad. Sad is not bad.

I love you, Harriet

February 12 (11 p.m.)

Dear Jerry,

I forgot to tell you how much I missed you by my side on Friday night, especially when our friends Mickey and Dinny held hands—it was so beautiful and loving. After returning home I turned on the TV (which I rarely do) to watch the opening ceremonies of the Winter Olympics in Torino, Italy. You and I rarely missed catching these events and I felt so lonely sitting on the couch watching it by myself.

Visiting Lee and Jim in their Florida home brought up so much sadness too—your death, their daughter's death and their close friend recently diagnosed with terminal cancer. Loss, loss, loss! The sadness stayed with me through today.

A blizzard in New York is keeping me from returning until Tuesday. Weather here is also cold and nasty and I feel like the weather. Guess I've got the blues…

Planning to visit my ninety year old friend Rose and then family while I have to stay in Florida has helped change my mood.

Today is Gary's 40th birthday and he and Shelley went to New York City for dinner and an overnight. Remember when I surprised you with a weekend in New York City to celebrate your 40th having shared that with Lee and Jim celebrating his 35th? Where do the years go? They fly like butterflies; you hardly see them, at least when life is good, healthy and loving. They flitter away quickly. But now time seems to be going more slowly especially on the sad and blue days.

I'm grateful for the life I shared with you; good, healthy and loving quickly lived, and now gone.

I love you, Harriet

February 14

Dear Jerry,

Two more swiftly flying days! Because of the extended stay I just participated in Grandparents' Day at Josh and Matthew's school. Remember how we shared that experience in years past? I wasn't the only single grandparent there though. I'm more aware of those things now. You would be so proud of both boys.

There was a second call to see if I changed my mind about having Valentine's Day dinner with them. I thought I had made my decision and reason clear. Believe it or not my plane arrived only one hour before my first private client and the massage was a perfect ending to a busy and stressful day. Valentine's Day was not such a big deal for us—two cards each, one serious and one funny. You always brought me flowers but you did that at other times throughout the year too. The holiday did not trigger emotions as surprising as that was to some people. What mattered was how much we loved and cared about each other and showed it every day of the year as "Harriet and Jerry". We were a team.

I love you, Harriet

February 15

Dear Jerry,

The reality of your death is always present. After a recent eye exam and now scheduled for cataract surgery in April, I immediately planned for who will drive me and who will pick me up. You would have been the one, as I was there for each of your numerous eye exams and surgeries, an important part of your diabetes health care.

Today was very full with my driving to Connecticut for a financial planning meeting that lasted 3 hours with lots of new ideas, new lingo, a list of things to do and decide upon.

In addition, in the evening I facilitated a bereavement group for adult children whose parent had died. One young man spoke so beautifully about his father who had also died suddenly from a heart attack and about having "no regrets". Didn't David also say that in his eulogy after thanking his parents for "teaching us all how to love. It is from their teachings and example that every time I said hello and goodbye to Dad it was with a hug and a kiss. And at the end of every conversation it ended with 'I love you'. Therefore I have no regrets!! I just want more!!!!!"

The young man described his loving father who was always helping everyone, teaching his children, being supportive of them, as well as loving his wife and being a role model for his son—all reminiscent of our family but we were more fortunate, I thought to myself. We had you longer in our lives. This son was only 21.

This day was filled with reminders that you are gone from our sight but not from our heart. Woke up with a headache this morning. I am not surprised but I hope writing to you, as well as two aspirin will alleviate the pressure in my head and the heaviness in my heart.

I love you, Harriet

February 18

Dear Jerry,

I'm flying home from visiting Aunt Marion in Austin, Texas. There were tears as I said goodbye knowing I probably won't see her alive again as she has end stage ALS. Goodbyes seem harder since you died and each goodbye is a reminder of the final goodbye to you. I know it's not once, but over and over again that I have to say goodbye to you and let you go. It's a normal part of the grieving process.

I'm glad I made the trip so I could share my feelings for her and how much she has meant to me. She has been a role model for me in many ways. Thanks for bringing her into my life. Interesting how I recall a trip to Arizona years ago to say "good-bye" to my Uncle Murray, before he died. These two were very special to me and I'm glad I spent quality time with them when they were healthy as well. I'm richer for these relationships.

I love you, Harriet

February 22

Dear Jerry,

So much is happening. So much to share! One meeting after another, taking care of the pets, visiting friends and relatives, traveling back and forth to Florida, paying bills and not to mention working! This busyness is helping me get through my grieving. But then again I have always thrived on activity. My hope is that I am taking time to grieve too. I don't want to be a "runner" as that would only abort my grief. This is my new "normal".

I forgot to mention that since I was going to Texas for only a couple of days I decided to drive my car to the airport rather than use a driver. I did not leave enough time. One, it was rush hour and two it was not that easy to get a parking spot near the terminal. The self check-in kiosk I chose didn't work. As it was a holiday weekend the security lines were particularly long. I was sweating the situation, I admit. I figured that you were laughing because you always wanted to leave plenty of time for plane travel and I always thought it wasn't necessary. You were correct. Now I know what the expression, "to catch a plane," means. I literally felt that is what I was trying to do.

Tonight was another Marriage Encounter meeting. Yes I still feel the need to attend. I wrote a long letter to you about how I believe that my parents influenced our life as a married couple in a positive way. I hope one day our children can say the same.

The meeting followed a long and busy day. It started with an

8:30 am meeting with the landscape designer for the Zen garden I am planning. I feel so excited about this creation. After much travail, I met with the trust lawyer and confronted him about what I believe has been incompetence. I felt better during and after the meeting. Once again I learned that honest communication is essential. Then I went to the bank and spent time getting help with changing our accounts. Having been invited to dinner at Joann and Philip's afforded me an opportunity to share my feelings about these meetings and my accomplishments. Now I am tired and spent but satisfied I am back on track dealing with these financial matters with clarity and intelligence. You did it for so many years. You always took care of me, of us! Now I am taking care of me.

I love you, Harriet

February 25 (7:00 a.m.)

Dear Jerry,

Shabbat Shalom. I went to services with Enid last night as Eddie was in the Far East. You know how much he loves to travel. You always appreciated that it saved you from having to travel to certain countries. I learned a secret from her that I can only share with you. When the location of the business changes Eddie will have what he needs to continue to work as long as he wants. That also will be true for Ben when he moves south. Once again, George proves to be a "mensch". I feel grateful that you ended your long career with the support, appreciation and respect from George.

In three days it will be six years since my dad's death. So long ago—yet so recent! The same is true for your six months. So hard for me to understand time. Perhaps that's why it took a genius like Albert Einstein to comprehend and formulate his theory of relativity.

Phoebe told me she had a clear dream of you and it was very funny. I was warmed to hear it but of course forgot the details.

I love you, Harriet

March 1

Dear Jerry,

Well, I did it! I stayed in the house all day until I organized all my papers for taxes, and then stood on line at the post office to mail them out.

Since February has 28 days tomorrow actually marks 6 months. Spring is coming. Gary has appeared depressed to me and recently Shelley confirmed that. David has shared that he has been pressured financially. Craig recites Kaddish daily in the privacy of his home and gets to Temple when his schedule allows it. It seems to me that the boys (our sons) are having a hard time balancing family, work and their grief and it has triggered mounds of emotions and pots full of tears. I also know that each one has to follow one's own way of grieving and coping. No different than with my clients. I can only listen and validate the normalcy of their grief. I cannot fix it for them. I can't for myself as well. Grief controls us.

Change of season and the six months are both additional triggers for normal grief reactions. Taking time to "be with you", miss you and experience all my feelings has been a luxury for me that the boys don't have. I lay in bed after waking and just "am"—no children to attend to, nobody to answer to. After a half hour I meditate, and/or write. I believe that's helping me balance with life's activities and my grief. I don't know for sure—I'm just following my gut. Pepper seems to be a comfort too as she cuddles with her paws placed on my face and I listen to her soft sweet meow and feel her licking (kissing) my eyes. When I looked at her papers from the vet it showed her birth date as approximately September 1. That coincides with your death. Could it be she was meant to come to me? I like to think that. She's sweet, loving and patient; all the qualities you possessed.

I love you, Harriet

March 4

Dear Jerry,

Every day this week I thought about it being six months since you physically left me and everyone else who knew and loved you; yet you are here. This is so evident from the dream Craig had, to lights flickering in their home, to the beautiful golf shots I had, and to the parking spot that miraculously appeared on the crowded street. You would have loved the last few days here in sunny Florida, sharing the beauty and peace with our friends Helene and Warren. Gary and Jane joined us for drinks one night. We laughed and nibbled cashews and pistachios and talked about you.

I still feel grateful for the peace I feel in my heart, the beauty that surrounds me and the love I receive from you, the children and special friends.

I love you, Harriet

March 5

Dear Jerry,

I sit here alone this morning feeling the warmth of the sun, hearing a plane, birds chirping, and the sound of a motorboat in the distance. Can you believe I slept 10 hours having gone to sleep at 9:30 last night? The remarkable thing is I dreamed about you. I realized it as I was waking. I never opened my eyes and while I had the thought that I should write it down as I probably would forget it otherwise, I didn't. I have forgotten some of the detail but overall I knew it was you as I listened to Craig and Amy share they were going to have a third child.

I remember saying, "Do you realize they will be ten years apart, Matthew and the next child?"

I remember looking at you and seeing your sweet face and how one eye was always slightly more closed than the other. As I was moving to a waking state, I recall thinking no way is it true that Craig and Amy are having another child and you couldn't really be here except in a dream. You died! I guess it takes a longer time for the heart and soul to realize the death as compared to the brain knowing that it happened.

I'm taking this morning to "do nothing." I have lots of options but I plan to reread a book I had bought for you.

I love you, Harriet

March 6 (8:30 a.m.)

Dear Jerry,

What was that all about? I flew home last night from Florida arriving about midnight. The bedroom panel for the alarm system was beeping in different rhythms, continuing on and off through the night. Not able to sleep I shut off the main panel but the upstairs panel continued to beep. Calling emergency service was a waste as they weren't available until 9 a.m. Then it stopped from the time I left the bedroom, about an hour ago. This did happen once before and the repairman found nothing wrong. Are you responsible for these electrical beeps? It is believed that dead people can and do communicate through electrical fields.

I finished reading Joan Didion's book, *The Year of Magical*

Thinking. It has been touted as an excellent book depicting her first year grieving after the sudden death of her husband. Little resonated in me as I don't believe I have denied the reality of your death. I didn't feel the need to get "proof" as she seemed to. However, I cannot compare myself to her as she was simultaneously dealing with a gravely ill daughter before and after the traumatic death of her husband. This is again another example of normal/unique grief. No two people grieve alike. Everyone has their own normal way of coping/grieving and their unique relationship with the deceased. In addition, it's important to look at other current stressors such as health, finances, responsibilities for young children or elderly family members as well as other losses and changes in one's life.

I feel peaceful and confident. I can manage my new life living alone. The support I have is amazing and the lasting love from you is always with me.

I love you, Harriet

March 9

Dear Jerry,

I've been visiting your sister daily since I came back from Florida as she is recuperating from some cosmetic surgery. I'm happy to be helping her. We widows have to stick together.

Pepper reminds me of you; "Jerry Vogel, never still; always seeking some new thrill." You always loved to share this quote from your high school yearbook with me.

I love you, Harriet

March 10

Dear Jerry,

Shabbat Shalom! It is so precious to hear Grant say that to me over the phone with his passionate young voice. I went to services tonight and felt embraced by the music and the familiar faces. All March birthdays were invited to the bimah for a blessing and so I went up too. I held back tears as I stood with the other people who were celebrating their birthdays. I knew you wouldn't be waiting for me in the pew to give me a kiss as in the past. There were tears; I felt sad and yet it was ok. The synagogue is both a trigger and a safe place to cry.

The songs I hear on the radio have been speaking to me too. For example, "Leaving You Softly," "My Beloved," and there was one giving me permission to find a new love. I'm not ready for that—no time, energy or desire. I think I have to go through a "year of firsts," first.

I love you, Harriet

March 14

Dear Jerry,

How surreal is this? I had a quiet weekend spending time with Sue and enjoying unusually warm winter weather. But around 4 p.m. on Sunday I received a call that Aunt Marion had died. Today is her funeral here on Long Island and my (our) home is set up for the Shiva, a reminder that we've hosted Shiva here many times, for our parents, an uncle, as well as for parents of friends.

Her children Steve and Marian and granddaughter Arielle flew in from Texas and are staying here. When they arrived we sat around the kitchen table until midnight talking and crying about Aunt Marion's last days, her life, our memories, and my last and lucky visit just weeks before.

We always were her "favorite niece and nephew" she said. Thank you for being my connection to this wise, articulate, dignified and funny woman.

I love you, Harriet

March 15 (7:00 a.m.)

Dear Jerry,

What a surprise when I just looked out my window to find Steve and Marian's rental car still in the driveway as they were supposed to leave by 6 a.m. for the airport. Their flight was delayed. I can hear the sounds of dishes being cleared from the dishwasher. They have been perfect houseguests. Their stay has been so relaxed and easy just as it was when I stayed in their home less than a month ago.

I'm sitting in bed thinking about yesterday, Aunt Marion's funeral. The day started with Steve, Marian, Arielle and I having breakfast together with more conversation about why we're together today. Marian and Arielle even wrote some letters to be placed inside the coffin. Then it was off to the cemetery, New Montefiore, where you are buried. It was emotional for me as well as for Gary, David and Tara, bringing back the memories of your funeral not so long ago. The rain cleared and the wind began to blow, all reminiscent of your Uncle Walter's funeral. I felt supported by Gary's arms. At first when asked to speak at this graveside service I didn't think I could, but then again I didn't think I could let this moment go by and not speak. I shared spontaneously what I had written to you—thanking you for bringing her into my life, the honored place she held as one of my role models, and that my first connection to Reform Judaism was when I attended her son Ben's Bar Mitzvah with you. Did you know Aunt Marion and Uncle Arthur met at a dance and danced the whole night the first time they met? Do you know two other people who met and danced away the first night they met? Well I do—I'm grateful I was one half of that couple 51 years ago.

I love you, Harriet

March 16 (11:30 p.m.)

Dear Jerry,

Yesterday after arriving in Florida I surprised Josh at his baseball game and saw Matthew hit a homerun at his practice.

Today I drove down to watch Amy play and win a tennis match for her team. She claims the tennis necklace I gave her for her birthday is her lucky charm but I know it's her skill and cool thinking. However, the highlight for today was going shopping with Amy to find a dress for Josh's Bar Mitzvah. When the saleswoman complimented Amy on how well she looked in the one she selected I began crying thinking that you will not be there. That's what's so sad.

I had just finished saying, "Dad will let you know how beautiful you look that day" when we heard a song playing in the background. I'm not kidding when I tell you it was "You Are So Beautiful To Me". I just knew you were there in that dress shop with us.

After school Josh and I drove up to our condo to play golf until dark and then I drove him back home.

You know how much I love to celebrate St. Patrick's Day but somehow it wasn't going to work for me on the 17th. So Craig suggested he and I go for dinner at Paddy McGee's tonight and I was able to enjoy delicious Irish food and a bottle of Guiness. Time alone with Craig, as is with anyone in the family, is always so special. I put on a lot of miles today but oh how lucky I am. It was a great day!

I love you, Harriet

March 20

Dear Jerry,

Spring! But it's cold here in New York. I had another whirlwind weekend in Florida, wishing you were with me, and our friends and family. Spent a lovely day with Barbara, having real conversation over lunch and strolling through Stuart where we found wall sconces that will be perfect for the living room. I think you would have liked them too. I hosted a Shabbat/ St. Patrick's Day dinner for the Lewits, Galperns and Coelhos. This was my second celebration of the holiday this week. You got it! The works: corned beef and cabbage, potatoes, my green salad dressing and Irish soda bread but I couldn't find a green challah.

Ed admitted he had a hard time coming into the condo for this was the first time for him since you died. He told us of his dreams of you, "clear, silent and real". Phoebe, Ed, Louise and David slept over and we spent a leisurely morning. We helped each other heal as we talked openly and honestly about you, sharing our individual feelings. While three of us played golf Phoebe and Ed went kayaking. This reminded us of the last great weekend together at Louise and David's home in the Berkshires just days before you died. The difference was you and David played golf and the rest of us went kayaking. We shared how you are and always will be with each of us. I hadn't realized until now how you were bigger than life when you were alive. Now you remain alive within each person you touched. The five of us went to my favorite restaurant, 11 Maple Street, to celebrate my upcoming birthday and I ate too much—I guess I was trying to fill the empty space inside me. I never will, especially with food.

Time spent with family at Matthew's birthday party had me sharing with Amy's sister-in-law our common grief journey as her father had died suddenly soon after you did. I shared my line for the week with her, "Sad is not bad."

I love talking about you, how you lived your life and of our life together. And now there's talk of creating a memorial to your memory at our local hospital, Winthrop University Hospital, to benefit children with diabetes and their families.

I love you, Harriet

March 22

Dear Jerry,

It's David's birthday today and he is having such a difficult time. He misses you so much. Everyone does!

As we mourn your death, plans are being made to honor your life. I attended a dinner bringing parents of children with diabetes and medical staff together to talk about creating an outreach program for Pediatric Diabetes Education at Winthrop University Hospital. Warren spoke of you so lovingly, gratefully and respectfully. I sat and listened to him and was so moved as he said you were a great man, one from whom he learned much. He also told those gathered that he had planned to ask you for your help in this endeavor prior to your death. He and Helene pledged a generous amount of money to start this fund. Wow! I don't have words to describe my feelings.

Last night I ended an eight-week bereavement group for adults whose parents had died. I felt proud and satisfied that I was able to focus just six months after you died, and no one in the group knew I was on my own personal grief journey. I plan to facilitate a spouse/partner group in April. I am pleased that I can continue my work counseling the bereaved. I believe it is because I am doing my own grief work. I also know you are guiding me. Thank you.

I love you, Harriet

March 23

Dear Jerry,

Here in Florida again—it's such a healing place and I've made the effort to keep my life going up north but come down here for extended weekends for additional healing. I flew down with Helene to celebrate our March birthdays. Remember how I used to smile every time we drove into Harbour Ridge always saying how lucky we were and never to take it for granted? Well driving into our community today I wasn't smiling but sobbing as I heard Johnny Mathis singing "The Twelfth of Never." How much do I need you???????? Monday I heard "I'll Be Seeing You" in all familiar places, and it's so true. Those small intimate moments, the everyday experiences... I think of you, speak of you and miss you more and more and more. When will it change?

Looking back I realized how much I have been overeating these past weeks, including having desserts for five days in a row! That has always been my negative way to deal with stress. Naturally, I gained weight and felt so uncomfortable and out of control. Grief can do that. As of yesterday I am aware and taking control. I remember the many times you helped me become aware of this pattern. For all those times, thank you.

I love you, Harriet

March 27

Dear Jerry,

A whirlwind weekend…what would you have said to that? After arriving from Florida I had 45 minutes to get ready for Carol and Stan's daughter's wedding and a sleepover at Phoebe and Ed's city apartment. The next day I met David, Tara and the girls for brunch, saw a show at Vineyard Theater, visited with Dan and Cori, had dinner at a local restaurant, and a visit with Peter in his New York pad. This was all good stuff and I had the energy to enjoy it all. I know you would not have loved this hectic pace as you had to adjust to the limitations of having diabetes on a continuous basis and sometimes you didn't have the energy when your blood sugar levels dropped.

My birthday is tomorrow. I'll miss your two cards on the kitchen table, your sweet smile as you wish me "Happy Birthday" with a special hug and kiss before you go off to work.

Everyone around me is making sure my birthday is filled with love, good wishes, cards, calls and plans but none can make up for your gift to me—yourself for 50 years.

I love you, Harriet

March 28

Dear Jerry,

I missed you at my side when I awoke today for you used to be the first to say "Happy Birthday" but soon after the birthday calls came in and flowers too from our children and grandchildren. I chose to start the day with a walk, a gift to myself, and heard the birds chirping and saw three little birds in a leafy area—three—and I knew that "every little thing gonna be all right."

I opened an envelope today, your bonus check, and that made for a beautiful present. The gift, however, is and always will be having been your wife, lover, friend, and sailing, tennis, golf, yoga and running partner and soul mate.

I love you, Harriet

April 3

Dear Jerry,

I haven't written lately but there's a lot to share. The other morning I reread the eulogies written by the boys and I cried and cried. Their expressions of love, their gratefulness, learned lessons, as well as their sadness and missing you triggered a river of tears in me.

Recently I saw Jill and Shelly, the mothers of our daughters-in-law Shelley and Tara, and was greeted with no words but with strong, embracing, loving hugs that spoke volumes. While those hugs were supportive they also triggered deep sadness once again as it was another acknowledgement of the reality of your death.

I had Jessie and Allie here for another sleepover and a concert in the city. They brought up memories of going to see the Paper Bag Players "together with Grandpa". I secretly wish you and I could still be taking them to shows and concerts together.

I have been staying in touch with your cousins Ben and Steve by phone and it feels good. It's a connection with Aunt Marion and you. I hope you are together again! I went to Temple with Sue where Aunt Marion's name was read aloud as it is customarily done for the period of sheloshim.

I am so fortunate to have so many people who care about me and show their empathy for my grief in so many different ways. And I know you are there too.

I love you, Harriet

April 4

Dear Jerry,

I'm catching up to you. I'm now 66 years old and had my first cataract surgery. Coincidentally the son of your eye doctor was the Fellow in the operating room with my eye doctor. I had a chance to talk with him, tell him about all the connections and how it was his father who performed laser surgery on your eyes in 1979 and saved your sight. I remember how Dr. Maris said he would always share your success story when he spoke professionally. All went well and three friends were great about driving me back and forth for the surgery and the follow up appointment.

I love you, Harriet

April 7

Dear Jerry,

I feel like I'm spinning out of control. Recovering from surgery was easy but I'm writing now from David and Tara's home as I'm watching their children while they're on vacation. In addition, I am working, planning for Seder and the family coming up from Florida for five days, making decisions and follow-up calls with the cemetery and monument company, with the landscape design company who will construct my new Zen garden, creating the service for the unveiling, arranging for food afterwards, anticipating our anniversary, paying bills and taxes, changing utility services in Florida for the summer season, and heading back to Westchester Thursday to bring the girls back to our home for the weekend. I'm tired just listing everything on this paper. Now I understand a friend saying she was tired just listening to me telling her what's been going on.

I did take advantage of the girls' babysitter and drove home to food shop, plant pansies and spend two hours uninterrupted organizing the service that I have felt motivated to create. I've been planning for your unveiling, having collected prayers, sayings and poems for a couple of months and I feel satisfied that it has all come together. I have counseled Jewish mourners that the unveiling is a "conscious funeral". The family has the control to decide the date, time, who will be there and the substance of the ceremony whereas there is little control over these factors for the funeral. Knowing this I want it to be sacred as well as meaningful for those who attend. It felt so sad rereading the service one more time, as I know full well the reason for all this is the simple fact that you died. If you were alive I'd be asking you to look it over and ask for your thoughts. I hope you will be proud of my efforts. I'm also hoping everyone will participate with impromptu sharing.

I love you, Harriet

April 9 (10:30 p.m.)

Dear Jerry,

What do I write on the eve of our wedding anniversary? I just finished writing a card to you as the tears dripped down my cheeks. I cried again when talking to Judy as she will be in Florida with her family for Seder and will not be with us at the unveiling, but they know the time and will stop and think of us at that set time. I cried again when Elaine and Steve called to acknowledge our anniversary and said they are waiting to hug me on Friday. I cried once again when Gary hugged me wishing me a peaceful day on his visit with the children.

Yes there's much pain and sadness but I had a distraction with the girls this weekend, especially when Riley came into my bed on your side and innocently asked, "Where's Grandpa?" When I answered, "He died," she repeated, "But where's Grandpa?" We talked for quite a while about death and Grandpa even though she will only be three in June. I know how important it is to use the real words with young children even though they are too young to understand the concept of death. In time they will be able to fit the words with the understanding of what happens when someone or something dies.

Pepper is now sitting by my side sensing my sadness as I write these words.

I plan to burn the anniversary card I wrote to you and sprinkle the ashes on your grave during my visit tomorrow. Do I make a date with you as we often did in the past for lunch or a matinee? What special times they were, just you and me, whether to make love or to speak of our love. We were so lucky. Our love was so special and that love has flowed to other couples like Yael and Bob who recently experienced a Marriage Encounter weekend.

I love you, Harriet

April 10 (11 p.m.)

Dear Jerry,

Our anniversary. The day is almost over and it didn't bring the pain I anticipated. I felt connected to you from my early morning thoughts and memories. First Pepper gave me lots of sandpaper "kisses" and cuddled next to me. Then there was the burning of the card/letter, then the songs I heard on the radio, including "The Incredible Memories of Sweet, Lovable You." How true! I cried driving to the cemetery and again at the grave which was my first time seeing the monument. After all the planning, when I saw your name, Gerald A. Vogel, the dates of your birth and death, Husband, Father, Grandpa, Brother, Friend along with the phrase, "Loved By All" inscribed on the granite, I cried for you. There were tears, not sobs. Then

I looked at the space next to your grave, the plot reserved for me. I was restless and couldn't stand still too long, so I walked around a bit and gathered thirteen stones to place on your foot-stone, one for each child, grandchild and me. I also found some larger stones to put on the family monument simply lettered with the name VOGEL. The song on the radio when driving away from your gravesite was "Cherry Blossom White" and I began to smile thinking of how many times we danced to that cha-cha and had so much fun doing it. Remember how I wanted our first wedding dance to be a cha-cha? However, I acquiesced to tradition and we struggled through a waltz. So many memories, so sweet, so special!

Tonight I went to "your" yoga class. All the "regulars" were there. That felt good. Another connection to you!

Back home again to receive more supportive phone calls. I also noticed the lack of some. "Sad but not bad." I have to be ok with it! How many times have I listened to mourners share that those who they thought were friends failed to call, visit or just stay in touch. This can be painful and sometimes I feel angry. I've been blessed with an outpouring of support from day one but I also have experienced the absence from some. Intellectually I know that it's not intended to be hurtful but rather it's the person's inability to cope. However, for the mourner and that's me right now it adds to the grief as we call this a secondary loss.

I ended the evening making charoset for Seder and after cleaning up got into bed to write to you. This was the first time in years that I had to go to the store and buy walnuts, samples of which you always brought home before Passover. Time for some rest now! Thanks for remaining in my life in unique and different ways.

I love you, Harriet

Fraternity Boat Ride, 1957

Our Wedding, April 10, 1960

The Family at Nephew Brian's Bar Mitzvah, May 1983

Craig and Amy's Wedding, November 1990

My Favorite Photo: Jerry and Our 3 Sons, 1994

Jerry and I Dancing at a Convention, 1996

The Family, Thanksgiving 2004

Jerry's Last Photo, August 2005

The Family at Jessie's Bat Mitzvah, May 2014

PASSOVER / UNVEILING

April 12 (7:30 a.m.)

Dear Jerry,

"Arise my beloved..." Oh, how I wish I could see you and hear you read that poem once again, and have you join us for Seder tonight. If you were alive you would have helped set the table. Phoebe and Ed were going to help me but instead are in Massachusetts coping with the tragic sudden death of her brother. (Craig, Amy and the boys will help when they arrive from the airport.) In the past before going to work you would be telling me what time you would be home to get ready and we would be going over some last minute plans for using the Haggadah. It's a beautiful spring day, birds chirping, flowers blooming—a time for rebirth and renewal. Just as there will be the customary answers to "Why is this night different than any other night?" the main answer for us this Passover is that you are not here, not alive. I am also choosing to make a change with the seating. For the very first time we will have a children's table. Can you believe Matthew has agreed to sit with the younger kids to "help out". Riley is all set with her question, a first for her this year. I'm sure I'll feel more anxious later as the day goes on and I miss your presence. I do know you will be here though if only "in memory and spirits" [sic] as Josh had written.

I love you, Harriet

April 12 (11:30 p.m.)

Dear Jerry,

This is the time we would be lying in bed, having put away the clean dishes, glasses, the chairs and tables, reviewing the evening. Why was this night different? Many things were different this year. First, your oldest son, Craig, sat in your seat and with his heart heavy with grief carried on the tradition of our family and our people. You would have been proud of his opening remarks. They were tender, poignant and moving and acknowledged the reality of why he was leading the Seder THIS year even though he as well as the other boys had done so in the past. He led the Seder against great odds having five young children between the ages of two and four as well as many adults who at times couldn't stay focused on the Haggadah. Matthew chanted and even played "Dayenu" on the piano. Josh's Hebrew and beautiful chanting was a foreshadowing of his upcoming Bar Mitzvah. It was a sad day and night. However, by feeling my grief (and not ignoring it) and crying openly I was at the same time releasing it and then able to enjoy my favorite holiday. Isn't that what I have repeatedly told the grieving about preparing for holidays? It is important to acknowledge the people who died by name before beginning to eat. I hope that was true for the others around the long table this year.

Whew! I survived our anniversary on Monday, Seder on Wednesday. I'm confident we will survive the unveiling on Friday, however sad and painful it will be.

I love you, Harriet

April 14 (6:45 a.m.)

Dear Jerry,

I have my window open and the birds' early morning sounds fill me with life and hope, the sounds of spring. And yet today we face another sad day. Today at 2 pm we will gather, a small group of family and close friends, to dedicate the monument at your gravesite to your memory. While I slept over eight hours, it was a restless sleep, with anticipation of a day that will bring me (us) back to the day of your funeral. My first memories flash back to my standing in a black outfit, walking slowly toward the hearse watching your coffin being moved to the gurney and saying aloud, "This is the real thing." I knew on some level this was reality; you had died, no longer breathing, would never touch me again with your tender but atrophied hands, never would look at me again with your sweet, soulful eyes, never would whisper "I love you" with your warm, caring voice.

I miss you so but I am living my life. I need you still but feel confident I can learn to do this without you. I yearn for you and know I won't be seeing you here and now. I will be patient to reunite with your soul one day. I will always remember you and speak of you. I will teach your grandchildren about you and include you in the things we do. I will continue to live my life in balance and in the moment. The tears rolling down my cheeks now will subside and they will begin again. When? I never know. And it's okay. It is sad but sad is not bad. I didn't have tears at the funeral. Will they be there at the unveiling? It's not important. What is important is the love we had for each other. "A gift from God," I would write in our numerous love letters. How grateful I am. Our love still shines with light to those who knew us as a couple. I still hear comments like that and it makes me smile.

I love you, Harriet

April 14 (Midnight)

Dear Jerry,

It was a perfect day—for unveilings that is. The weather was symbolic. Prior to and during most of the service it was raining quite hard but it stopped at the end just as the theme of the service turned from memory and grief toward hope and healing. It was a small gathering of close family and friends, in contrast to the hundreds who attended your funeral. That's what I wanted. Jessie and Allie were present this time with their precious innocent smiles as they moved about touching and leaning on the tombstone. You would have loved seeing them dressed in skirts. Riley and Grant were back at the house with their nannies (not me this time). Your sister, our children and the two oldest grandsons read parts of the service that I had created, one befitting you.

I will always remember seeing Allie, without a single word, put her arms around her dad to comfort him as he knelt by your grave sobbing. It was very hard for the boys to see your name on the stone for the first time. I was grateful that this was not my first time.

Friends, huddling under a mix of colorful umbrellas spoke impromptu from the heart. The weather began to change from rain to drizzle to a bit of sunshine. The text of the service went from sadness to healing. We went from sadness, tears and sobs to happiness, smiles and even laughter at times.

Michael and Sally along with their boys, in from Israel, had been caught in traffic driving from Philadelphia. They finally arrived and had their long awaited "private time with you".

Back to our house to continue remembering, talking and living. I gave a watch from the golf tournament to each of your close male friends, Ed, David, Steve, and Bill and they were blown away. After almost everyone left it was time for Kabbalat Shabbat prayers and all the Vogels and Klein-Katzs shared the blessings over candles, wine and challah. Life does go on and holidays are to be celebrated even when experiencing the pain of grief. And now it was time to eat again. Jews do this very well. Josh once again helped me clean up and the house is ready for tomorrow's breakfast for nine of us.

Pepper is already asleep as well as Mushroom. I'm going to close my eyes as well now.

I love you, Harriet

April 17

Dear Jerry,

I slept from 8:30 pm to 7 this morning and then rested for another 30 minutes with Pepper. I actually got into bed at 8 pm attempting to read the NY Sunday Times, a luxury I've had little time for lately. To say I was exhausted is an understatement! It was both a physical and emotional depletion of energy. However, I am grateful for my sleep and generally it is uninterrupted and reenergizing.

Yesterday I was up and ready to play golf with Josh at 7 am. Mike the caddy master gave us the go ahead since Josh was flying home later that day even though the rules state that a minor cannot play before a certain time. As this was the time you and I had so enjoyed playing a round of golf together, I felt closer to you and also was aware of the beauty of the golf course at this early hour. Josh too had a good time especially because he had some really good shots. After I drove Craig and Amy and the boys to the airport I went out for another nine with Helene and Warren. We have had an unusually warm week for mid April in New York. I even went out Thursday by myself as a balancer between Seder and the unveiling. I wish I had a count of how many golf rounds you and I had enjoyed together. I do remember that I chose to take up golf in college over tennis when we were dating as that was one of your favorite sports and I had a hunch I might be spending my life with you.

Saturday evening Gary, Shelley, David and Tara came back to Long Island as we planned to go to the Club for dinner. I asked them to come to the house first as I had something important to share with them. I brought them and Craig and Amy up to our bedroom and showed them your basket of books that rested next to your side of the bed. They were all books on self-improvement. I told them about your work with the psychologist to overcome your anxieties and her words to me after your death helping me understand the symbolism of these anxieties as your fear of death. Then I showed them the book you kept next to your bed, *The Next Place*. My hope was that they too would believe you are at peace. I don't know if they do. I do! And I am at peace too although I miss you so.

I love you, Harriet

April 19 (12 a.m.)

What a contrast between Sunday night and tonight. After that emotional and physically demanding week instead of tackling bills and other paperwork I binged on more sweets and quickly hit the sack very early. Tonight however, after work and seeing two clients I lit the holiday candles to end the week of Passover, said the blessings over bread (matzah) and wine and lit six yahrzeit candles, one each for your parents, mine, one for all the friends and relatives we want to recall as was our family ritual and one for you. Then I sat down to a lovely dinner. I felt good about myself and like you used to do, went into the den, put on the TV and proceeded to take care of paying bills, balancing several accounts and organizing my paperwork. There are lots of decisions I have to make, for example, choosing a new sprinkler company, arranging for carpet cleaning, power washing the house, select lighting and fencing for the backyard, and on and on. It was easier when we shared those responsibilities. I am grateful I have the strength, intelligence and interest to do all I am doing. You've been a great role model for me.

I love you, Harriet

April 21 (midnight)

Dear Jerry,

Just received a beautiful letter from my sister acknowledging my courage since your death. I realized I'd never fully acknowledged the courage she has shown facing her life struggles so I called her tonight to share my thoughts and feelings.

Yesterday I went to do errands and shop at Costco. "That was a big bill," I thought as I began driving home with my car laden with food and things for the house. I thought how odd…what was all this for if you aren't here? In the trunk and backseat were assorted food items for me, kitty litter for the cats, golf and tennis balls and mats for the house. Then my feelings changed to gratefulness that I have the desire to keep life going for me.

I even went shopping after work and bought some nice clothes wishing you could see me in them. You always loved me to model any new clothes that I bought. I think this was the first time in about a year I had any interest for new clothes. Tomorrow I will go through the remainder of your clothes and prepare them for donation. I recognize the desire to keep involved in life. For now though it's time to sleep.

I love you, Harriet

April 22

Dear Jerry,

After months of failing health Ed's mom Shirley died. Everyone, including Shirley, was waiting a long time for this death. There I was crying again after I got the call as I felt such sadness for all the recent deaths. New loss always triggers old grief.

Phoebe and Ed were phenomenal each in their own ways loving her, caring for her and accompanying her on her final journey. And I hope to continue to accompany them on their journey of grief. When I learned they were going to Temple Friday night for her brother's death I told them to be at my house at 6:15 for Shabbat dinner and then we would go to services together. They were there for Sue and me the first Friday after Shiva. Little did we realize both Benson, Phoebe's brother, and Shirley's names would be read from the pulpit the same night. Lois and Stu, Bea and Harry, our Marriage Encounter 'family' and other long time Temple members joined too. We were their community surrounding them at this sad time. Jackie and I will prepare the Shiva and I will host some of Ed's out of town relatives. Once again the timing is ideal as I did not have plans to be away for this weekend and can help them. That's what friends do.

Going through your clothes was sad too reminding me of the times you wore this or that. I'm hoping Ed will finally accept your handsome navy blazer. It has been months since I offered it to him. I plan to keep your yellow cashmere sweater to warm me when I feel chilled in the cool weather.

What memories I hold! I just said to Judy, " I have a lifetime of loving memories to hold onto with one hand as I reach out for my future with the other."

Yesterday I loved hearing the song, "Just Came By To Say I Love You". It was just what I needed to hear. Thank you.

I love you, Harriet

April 23 (8 a.m.)

Dear Jerry,

I slept fitfully last night. It's pouring, it's cold, windy and I wish I could stay in bed today, writing, reading and sleeping but I can't. I have houseguests and we all have to get ready to go to Shirley's funeral. It brings it all back—missing you, and you missing all that's been going on in our lives.

I love you, Harriet

April 26 (6:30 p.m.)

Dear Jerry,

I wish you were here now. You were supposed to be taking this trip with me to see Cathy. I am sitting in the JetBlue food court at a Japanese restaurant sipping hot sake and waiting for the steamed edamame that I ordered. Yes I am heading to Seattle and then to Langley where she lives. I'm sad you are not coming with me but excited to see Cathy and be embraced by her love and healing powers. I have no other expectations but to be nurtured by her unconditional love. She is my friend, mentor and grief counselor all in one. How timely is this, coming only three weeks after our wedding anniversary date. She will be a gift for my soul. She flew in during Shiva and now I am going there to celebrate her birthday and fulfill our promise to visit her in her new home.

I love you, Harriet

April 27 (10 p.m.)

Dear Jerry,

Cathy is watching "ER" on TV and I am writing to you of a beautiful day spent with her touring Deception Pass and several tulip farms. She has a beautiful view from the house where sometimes whales are spotted. I know why she is so happy here. I am too.

I love you, Harriet

April 29 (10 p.m.)

Yesterday was another glorious day on Whidbey Island. We dined at a restaurant located on the edge of a cliff overlooking the water to celebrate Cathy's birthday. The food was yummy and the wine divine. Cathy said it was a perfect birthday and I was her best present. I felt the same way about being with her. She, too, has been a gift in my life.

I Love You, Harriet

May 2

Dear Jerry,

Got home yesterday at 7:45 a.m. having taken the "redeye". Then I went into regular mode for a typical Monday workday.

How excited I was this morning as the crew arrived to start work on the new Zen garden! I left for work to return at 2:00, thrilled to find a crew of four men laying electric cables and another crew of eight workers pulling out old bushes and planting new ones. And then driving back to the office I cried—the realization that you weren't going to share this new garden with me. I cried once again when I shared these feelings with Lorraine back at work.

I love you, Harriet

May 8

Dear Jerry,

So much to tell you and I don't know where to begin.

The garden is "growing." It's my new creation. I am pleased with my decision to try something new, rather than replicate the old! For me it's a symbol of this new chapter in my life. It's part of my healing.

Last Thursday we held our annual Hospice Memorial

Service. I was asked if I wanted to have your name read and hang your photo on our "Tree of Life" as do the family members who attend. I declined as I didn't want to use that venue for remembering you. My professional role is to support the hospice families and not process my grief. I grieve for you daily in many ways. For example, when I spent the day in Massachusetts at a memorial for Phoebe's brother. It reminded me there is still so much grieving to be done—your death, and the many other deaths of family and friends this last year.

I am ever grateful for my health and awareness and having had you in my life so long. I know you are with me morning and night. I may be alone but I am not lonely. I may be sad at times but sad is not bad.

I love you, Harriet

May 10

Dear Jerry,

My days seem to roll by so fast and I guess that's a good sign. I'm productively busy and engaged in life.

I'm definitely relating to the spouse bereavement group I'm facilitating on Monday nights. As I listen to them share during the sessions I hear some of the same feelings and thoughts I have been having. They're young, articulate and some have experienced the same sudden traumatic death of a spouse, some had excellent relationships, some are already using a variety of coping skills and some are struggling with their feelings and their new journey. I learn from each and I am validated for my normal/unique grief. Of course they are not aware of my personal loss.

I came home Monday night from work to see a completed new Zen garden. I was thrilled seeing the stones, plantings and water fountain all in place.

The next morning I got up early to see it in its entirety in natural light—a symbol of creation, new beginnings, nature, God, peace, a connection with you in a new way since the idea was conceived by David after your death during the week of Shiva. He has offered to paint the porch walls and lay new carpeting, his way of supporting all this change and me. I am so blessed to have the love and emotional and physical support from each child.

I gave Shelley and Tara their birthday gifts along with my messages explaining that I had bought their bracelets in Florida while attending the Convention in January. It was my way of including them back in January when I attended the convention along with their husbands. They are marked with the eye symbol to ward off evil but I know you are protecting them as well.

I went to a conference on "Death and Dying" and was touched by a poem read which reminded me of how you were ready to take your final journey.

Lee told me she and Christine went to a medium. I had thought

I might do it back in March for my birthday. I'm wondering why I haven't.

I enjoyed a visit from my cousins, Harmon and Beverly, who were in from Cincinnati visiting her sister. What I thought would be an hour's visit became 2 ½ hours as we covered everything from your funeral to the fact that four adult cousins in the family were widowed within one year. Harmon was quite open about his loving feelings for you and impressions of your funeral. This was another opportunity of remembering and letting go, a healing time for me.

I love you, Harriet

May 18

Dear Jerry,

A week later—so much has happened, so much to share. I have so many feelings inside.

I flew to Florida—spending intimate time again with Louise and David. We talked and talked and cried and cried some more. The time with them was sad but peaceful, loving and supportive. I shared with David how comfortable I feel with him, especially when he openly cries with me. The next morning he commented on how what I shared connected us even more. Isn't that what was our strength, Jerry? It was open and honest communication of our feelings. After sleeping there, we played 18 holes of golf the next day. Louise is playing much better and she loves her new driver, a birthday present from a few "girls". She said she wished you could see her now.

I picked up Josh and Matthew, to take them to Orlando's Discovery Cove to swim with the dolphins, a birthday present Matthew selected after much research and planning. He chose a restaurant in Stuart rather than the closer Palm City Grill the first night because, "That's where Grandpa and you took us after the show we saw." He loved the history of the bank robbery and the taste of the sensational French fries.

We slept at our condo and left for Discovery Cove in Orlando very early in the morning. The weather was spectacular, the setting beautiful and it was a very well run operation. However, after all the talk and planning Matthew was the only one who didn't want to snorkel after spotting a stingray. He did enjoy the float down the "lazy river" which took us through an aviary. How cool was that! Along the way the boys commented about a man that reminded them of Grandpa. At 4:00 we had our encounter with "Rascal", our dolphin. Then we headed to Sea World where Matthew went on a ride by himself, a ride you would never have gone on in your adult life. When watching the "Shamu Show" I was reminded of our trip to the Seaquarium in Miami when we babysat for Eitan and Emanuelle. So much reminds me of you and what we have done. We ended a great birthday celebration by having a late dinner in a fast food restaurant, a perfect choice for Matthew. It wouldn't have been for you. By 11 we were back in our condo for much needed sleep.

The next morning after the boys helped me bring in the porch furniture to prepare for hurricane season, we drove to their house. It was Mother's Day. Brunch, flowers and cards were waiting for me. So were Craig, Amy, Gary, Shelley, Allie and Grant. Later Brian, Gila and their children joined us and we all headed to the beach. Being with children and grandchildren, nieces and nephews on Mother's Day was a good distraction and the holiday did not feel sad for me.

A flight home to New York that evening brought me a most powerful experience. The person sitting next to me turned out to be a friend from elementary school days and then again in college—how bizarre that she recognized me - and we found out we had many common experiences. She too is widowed, is a social worker/grief counselor and her home address has the same three digits as mine. Her name is Bayla and I plan to see her again. She remembered you and I remembered her late husband Harry from our college years. I even suggested that perhaps we could meet with Ruth who I reconnected with in February after many years apart. After all it was the three of us back in Laurelton when we were in elementary school. And now we all were widows, have had careers in counseling and could be open and supportive in our sharing.

I deplaned carrying two roses, one each, given to me by Craig and Gary. I came home on a high and then saw my Mother's Day gift from David. He had painted the porch and laid new carpeting. What love was showered on me this Mother's Day! Was it more because you died? Was it more than I remember of past holidays? It doesn't matter. I realize it reinforced how special our children are and how they learned to love me by the way you loved and treated me. I only hope they do that for their children.

By the way, David told me that he found working on the porch very emotional and therapeutic as he recalled memories of helping you prepare the porch years ago. While I was away the outdoor lighting installation was completed and next weekend I will paint the porch furniture as I do yearly to give it a fresh look. I wish you could share this new backyard with me.

Creation is a healing force after the death of a loved one. Revelation is new people being revealed to me since you died, for example my two closest friends from my childhood, Ruth and Bayla. It is also revelation of new feelings and realizations since your death. For example, I have been learning about synchronicity, the timing of words, ideas, people and experiences. The synchronicity of life that has been revealed to me has me more convinced than ever that there are no accidents and everyone and everything is connected whether alive or dead. Marcia and I have talked about relief and freedom. There is freedom, freedom from caring for sick spouses.

Interesting that the three major holidays teach us these values; Sukkot - creation, Passover - freedom, Shavuot - revelation.

I love you, Harriet

May 20

Dear Jerry,

When Lorraine came to the house Thursday night she told me you welcomed her with a gust of wind that blew residue from the trees off the roof.

"It was momentary," she said, and we were wondering, was it really you?

Mother's Day continued for me as I received three orchid plants from the children, as well as a beautiful thank you card from Josh for our time in Orlando.

Judy and I spent yesterday planning for our trip to Israel and looking for dresses for the respective Bar Mitzvahs of our grandsons, Jacob and Josh. We visited your grave, as she wasn't able to be there for the unveiling. I sent her home with a copy of the service and of course she was moved to tears as was Cathy when she recently read it. Judy misses you as well as I and we always joke that she's known you longer than I have, having known you in high school. How fortunate I am to have these special people in my life as they too loved you and therefore they too miss you and mourn for you. "The spirit of love that binds us in life is indestructible in death." Corban Addison wrote that in *The Garden of Burning Sand.*

I am not alone in my life. I am not alone in my grief.

I love you, Harriet

May 21 (7:45 a.m.)

Dear Jerry,

I felt tired when starting my day yesterday. A bit blue and not in the mood to do any paperwork and procrastinated some writing I had planned to do. I actually changed from decaf to regular tea thinking I needed something to help me feel differently. Reluctantly, I decided to start the day by moving out things in the garage so I can have the garage power washed. Afterwards, I ended up spray painting the porch furniture even though the breeze was increasing knowing full well that wasn't the best time. The sun began peeking it's head out and I was feeling hopeful again, thinking I can handle all that is needed to keep this house going, the outer house, our home and the inner house, that is my heart and soul. By 1 o'clock I was tired but happy and lay down on the porch couch and thought of you doing the same after a Saturday round of golf with your friends. Physical work or exercise is such a great way of changing one's mood. Of course if you were alive and we were doing the house chores together it would have been a snap to get started and we'd be finished in half the time.

Then it was into the shower to get ready to attend the church wedding ceremony of my former client whose husband died on 9/11. The reception wasn't to begin for several hours so in between I visited Jane and Barry whose daughter, Amy, was to be married the next day, went shopping, stopped at a local dress shop to try on some dresses as possible choices for Josh's Bar Mitzvah, stopped at Linens and Things to make a return and bought a new tablecloth, matching napkins and coordinating place mats for the porch table. In my travels I also saw, purchased and brought home a bistro table with two chairs for the new garden. Having a convertible with the top down and the help of the store manager I was able to fit it all in the car. Of course I couldn't stop at that point. I ironed the wrinkles out of the new tablecloth, placed the nick knacks all around, added some green plants and at 7:00 o'clock was able to say I had a wonderful day. I felt satisfied. You would have been proud of me and would have loved how the porch looks. I'm excited to share this with everybody who will be visiting the house but of course you really are the one I would love to share it with.

When Linda came by to say hello, she helped carry the new table and chairs from the car saying, "Jerry would have loved the new garden."

I'm so grateful for the friends who have the courage to speak your name.

I then washed and dressed to go to the wedding reception. It felt good to dress up in a cocktail dress and while I missed you saying how pretty I looked, I did get acknowledged by one of the staff at the venue and smiling back, I nodded and said, "Thank you".

It was the second wedding I went to alone and it was fine. I danced with the bride and two male guests and I must admit I enjoyed the feeling of dancing at a happy event. When I danced with the bride she looked amazed that I had the moves. Remember she only knew me these last few years as her grief counselor. Once again I was reminded of us as I watched an older couple dancing and swaying to the music with style and grace.

That all took place yesterday! Today is a beautiful day (a better day to have spray painted) and I am going to see David play squash in Brooklyn Heights, do some paperwork, walk later with Linda and probably have a light dinner in honor of her 65th birthday.

I'm alive and well and have much to be grateful for.

I love you, Harriet

May 22 (7 a.m.)

Dear Jerry,

Yesterday I spoke with Kris and we firmed up plans for my visit to Michigan this summer. We talked about the synchronicity of things happening since your death. Yesterday was another example of that as the day unfolded. The early morning was beautiful and I sat in the new garden before getting dressed to head into Brooklyn. Drove with the top down, hit no traffic and easily found a parking space facing Hotel St George. Didn't we go there to swim in their famous indoor pool during our dating years? After David won his first squash match of the tournament we took time to stroll along the Promenade with its breathtaking views of the NY skyline including the Statue of Liberty and Ellis Island but minus the Twin Towers. The day continued to flow when I returned home. Linda came by and gifted me with a beautiful Japanese bell she bought at the Morikami Gardens in Boca Raton. Just this morning I had hung the bamboo chimes given to me by Shelly. Everyone is honoring my new Zen garden. Linda and I spent and enjoyed about four hours of relaxed time together including a walk, wine and delicious food made by both of us. I told her this is how you and I might have spent a late spring Sunday afternoon. She said it was a high compliment. She claims she often feels your presence. However, I only see your face when looking at photos. I am beginning to lose the clarity of how you looked.

I am grateful that I am comfortable in my home, garden, car and wherever. Now I really have to catch up with paperwork, pay bills and write an important letter. I have a full day scheduled including donating the remainder of your clothes and going to the DMV to change the registration for the Audi.

Stay close. I love you. Harriet

May 26 (11:30 p.m.)

Dear Jerry,

The last three days were filled with so many emotions.

Wednesday Sue and I had breakfast at a diner when I gave her a check from you. Of course I had written a note to her regarding your gift and we both cried as she read it.

At night I was at the Garden City Hotel for a dinner honoring Warren. It was a great tribute to him and an honor for me to be supporting him.

On Thursday I was out with Phoebe and Ed to celebrate her birthday. I shared with them that I have no envy for other people, places or things right now. I am peaceful and grateful for having had you in my life. Easy words to write but emotional to feel and share!

Still frustrating trying to solve the security system beeping at random times. Maybe it's more than you trying to say hello to me.

Today I took the time to write a thank you to each of the boys for a most memorable Mother's Day. I also wrote a note accompanied by a check to Craig and Amy to be used for the upcoming trip to Israel. I am clear that you and I would have agreed to do that. I only wish I had had you here to talk about it. It takes more time and thought when doing it by myself.

Judy and I met in Manhattan to continue to look for dresses for our grandsons' Bar Mitzvahs. I felt doubly lucky as I found two possibilities. One is a keeper for sure. It's pretty, feminine and classic yet stylish. Being with Judy was special as it always is. To think we have been so close since college, even chose each other as godparents for two of our sons and now we are sharing the excitement and preparation for the upcoming Bar Mitzvahs of our firstborn grandsons. I also anticipate a meaningful pilgrimage to Israel with her this July. We talked about that too and about you, of course.

I loved telling Josh about my new dress I look forward to wearing at his Bar Mitzvah. As usual his reaction was so sweet telling me he will love it.

I made the final payment for the new garden. The new garden is not only beautiful; it's peaceful. It gives me what you gave me; comfort, security and peace.

I love you, Harriet

May 27 (11 p.m.)

Dear Jerry,

I just returned from a festive night at NSCC; the Memorial Day dinner. It was held outdoors with the usual delectable seafood menu of lobsters, steamers and all the sides. There was a fireworks display over Hempstead Harbor, all reminiscent of many special nights we shared at the country club for 25 years. I was greeted warmly by many of the members and I felt comfortable being there as a single woman seated with Jane and Gary and their friends Bonnie and Larry.

Earlier in the day I had Sue and Debbie for breakfast, followed by a drive up to Connecticut to visit Gary and Shelley and the kids in their new home on their wedding anniversary. Everything looks beautiful. On the way back I thought how prior to your death we would have been talking in the car about how special the visit was and how proud we are of the children and their achievements, but today I thought about it all by myself.

I love you, Harriet

May 29

Dear Jerry,

I had a surprising but wonderful phone call from Dr. Sussman, your cardiologist, during the week. I remember well that summer Sunday night waiting in the ER back in 1988 after bringing you to Winthrop Hospital because your symptoms of nausea, Alice told me, could be a sign of a heart attack. My memory of the man approaching me, as I sat yearning to hear the diagnosis was simply a stomach virus, was that he was young, tall and handsome. He introduced himself and quickly told me how serious the situation was, saying we would have to see what happens over the next 48 hours. Today he was checking up on Craig, the other boys and me. How special is that! That attests to who you were in life. Even your doctor misses you and is concerned about your family.

Not only did I participate in the evening festivities for Memorial Day, yesterday I played in the annual Jack and Jill golf tournament. I had a male partner as is required but it wasn't the one I wanted and had for all those past years. I miss you.

Today was unique and nostalgic as I met with Ruth and Bayla in Bayla's apartment in Manhattan. We talked for hours as we had so many years to catch up on. It was our first time together since probably 8th grade, all a result of your death and a chance meeting on an airplane. First I received the letter from Ruth after your death and then I met Bayla on the plane after spending Mother's Day weekend in Florida. We never left the apartment even though we had planned to take a walk around the Upper West Side. We talked nonstop for seven hours at which time I said I had an appointment that night. It was Monday and I wanted to get to the night yoga class having missed my usual morning session.

Earlier in the day I took my first big bike ride of the season. After a cool spring it feels like summer today and once again I wish you were here to enjoy it with me.

I love you, Harriet

June 2

Dear Jerry,

I find myself procrastinating with my paperwork as well as calling to make an appointment to see a medium. I'd rather plant flowers, clean up the house, or fix a broken item. I guess these physical activities are more healing than the bill paying and they don't remind me of your absence as bill paying does. But, I do pay the bills, one by one. Just yesterday a widower in one of my bereavement groups shared that he plays tennis rather than do his paperwork, but eventually he too, does it. I did reassure him that the tennis is a distraction as well as

healing and therapeutic. However, I am satisfied that just yesterday I mailed out five copies of my workshop, "Coping With
The High Holy Days After The Death Of A Loved One" in
hopes of sharing it with rabbis and educators. I have chosen
to dedicate it to your memory. This workshop offered at my
hospice agency annually has been a successful tool for helping Jewish families look ahead to the challenges of celebrating
the Jewish New Year while grieving. I look forward to some
responses. I'll keep you posted.

I love you, Harriet

SHAVUOT / FATHER'S DAY

June 3

Dear Jerry,

It's Shavuot today and like on the two other major festivals I
went to Yizkor services at 7:15 a.m. yesterday—and once again
found that the moment the organ music started, I became teary.
It's a safe place to slow down and feel my sadness. Strange that
the night before when I lit the yahrzeit candles I had no emotional reaction. After services I connected with Linda whose
husband, Howard, died in December of brain cancer. We talked
about the two of you, our grief journey and our families. We
made a decision to bike together in a few weeks.

I was happy that it was a rainy day as it made it easier to focus
on paperwork, followed by errands to the bank and post office.
Then Joan and Steve hosted me once again for Shabbat dinner and conversation with their friends, the Goldbergs, with
whom I have so many connections of people (synchronicity

once again). The five of us went to Temple for a special service dedicating the new building. Your name was starred in the printed listing of those who had died after pledging to support this campaign. All donors were called to the bimah and I cried for you not able to accompany me. I know it was because of your hard work, your dedication and your interest that allowed us to participate in the support of this new building. I stood there for both of us and I'm reminded how perfect it was to have your funeral at Temple Sinai, a "second home for our family", as Craig shared in his eulogy.

He said, "We are in the right place now. I'm standing in the spot where 28 years ago this weekend I celebrated my Bar Mitzvah with Dad, Mom, our family and our friends. We've shared many joyous occasions here and I've sat next to him for Yizkor and recited the Kaddish so many times."

Can you believe that when I came home I followed up with more bill paying and solving computer snags, purchased plane tickets for Jacob's Bar Mitzvah in Florida, as well for David's family for Josh's upcoming Bar Mitzvah, looked for old bills to resolve a garage floor problem as well as a gutter problem. I worked until 1 a.m. I am working hard to keep the house in good repair. I love this space and have for so long (35 years). To me it's also about honoring you who felt that way and all we did as a team.

I love you, Harriet

June 10

Dear Jerry,

Shabbat Shalom – one week later and while I haven't written, you have been on my mind, in my heart, and on my tongue throughout the week whether in my silent thoughts, gathering names of mediums to make an appointment to hopefully connect with you, to having bereaved parents at a reunion ask about me and how I have been coping, to talking with Judy about the memorial plaque I intend to purchase, to conversation with Phoebe and Ed last night at our dinner prior to going to see a show at Vineyard Theater about their missing you, to Jessie when we talked about going to the beach Sunday to celebrate Riley's birthday and when I had asked her, "Who else was there last year?" Jessie answered, "Grandpa", to the message left on the machine by Lee and Jim saying they received a copy of Winthrop University's newsletter showing a photo of you and me at a past Opera Night fundraising event to time spent with Sally Sunday through Monday talking about you, reminiscing and crying.

How could it be any different? We were so connected. And I am so grateful for all the friendships that have remained connected too. Some of the songs I have been hearing on the car radio lately have significance for me, always connecting you and me.

I love you, Harriet

June 12

Dear Jerry,

Today is Riley's third birthday and you were missed yesterday at her beach birthday party. It was a beautiful sunny day. I biked with the girls on the boardwalk, walked to the ocean, collected shells, talked about you, had cupcakes, sang "Happy Birthday" and when I asked Riley, "Who is not here today?" she answered, "Grandpa Cashew," her designated name for you. I've been feeling sad this whole week. I cried on the drive to the beach and on the way back. I knew going home alone to the empty house would not have altered my feelings so I called your sister and found that I could stop at her home for an impromptu dinner on her backyard deck. We both loved the spontaneity and the chance to talk and cry together. We both miss you. It helped.

I love you, Harriet

June 15 (10 p.m.)

Dear Jerry,

Where do I begin? Today was a very powerful and healing day. I attended a conference called "Spirituality and Healing" at my alma mater, Hebrew Union College. It was sponsored in part by the Shira Ruskay Hospice and Palliative Care Center, named in memory of a colleague of mine. I loved being back at the school as well as seeing people I knew and meeting new professionals in the field. The keynote speaker, Joan Borysynko, is well known in this field and she was very inspiring. Debbie Friedman led us in song and she always moves people with her music and her heart. I not only reconnected with people who attended the conference but I reconnected with you, my nanny, Shira, and several others who have died but had been part of my life's journey.

One of the workshops I attended dealt with moving on after a spouse dies. I am not totally sure if it meant more to me personally than professionally. It's too early too distinguish. I just know it was important for me to be present. After this meaningful day I headed to Judy and Kenneth's apartment as planned and shared my day's experiences and feelings with them. Again it is so important to have supportive and non-judgmental friends.

It's been a tearful week for me once again but sad is not bad. I'm not totally surprised that I've been feeling sad lately as it's coming close to 11 months since your death. Part of my responsibility as a grief counselor has been to educate. It seems that there are significant times in the calendar year that may affect grieving people more intensely and they are 3, 6, 9 and 11 months after the death.

I'm sad and coping and doing what I need to do. For example I received calls from past clients, particularly widows, checking up on me. That's a twist! It all helps.

Last night I let go of more tears viewing once again the movie "Live and Become" about an Ethiopian boy given up by his mother to an Ethiopian Jewish woman, whose child has died, so he could be airlifted to safety and a new life. All about loss and grief, profound for me.

Mailed Father's Day cards to each of the boys with my personal message including a check in the amount you designated for each in your will. Three hours at the financial planners' office also emphasized the reality of your death as they gathered information and I signed numerous papers to start the process of moving monies in order to follow a concise plan for my future.

I sit alone on the porch. Breezes are blowing. The temperature is comfortable. I hear a plane overhead and cars whizzing by on Roslyn Road and it's my "mik dash m'at" (small sanctuary). Wish you could be here!

I love you, Harriet

June 17 (8 a.m.)

Dear Jerry,

I continue to listen to music on the car radio. The songs I have been hearing as well as tuning in to the U.S. Golf Open at Winged Foot this year speak directly to my heart and the memories of my mind. I am crying now just reliving my reactions. A phone call just came from David. He too was crying, he said, recalling times you had taken him to the Open or talked about or played a round of golf together. Wasn't it your dad who taught you the game, which then became our family game? David did attend the U.S. Open yesterday, followed by a round of golf, this time without you.

Craig and I finally connected on the phone and shared, first time in a long time. We cried together as he had opened my card and told me he too was triggered when on the golf course on Saturday. The boys are away at camp he said and so he is missing his father and his sons all at the same time.

Bill and Alice invited us to come to Massachusetts for the traditional Father's Day barbeque, one we had shared for many years when they lived on Long Island. I told them I would leave the decision to the boys as to what they wanted to do on their first Father's Day without you. They wanted to follow that ritual so we drove to their new home in the Berkshires for the day, all except Craig and his family who naturally remained in Florida. I took time to talk with Bill one on one. I shared openly even though I had to be confrontational. It was meaningful for me to express myself. I hope it was for him to hear what I had to say.

Also saw and spoke with Barry who having been widowed since Adrienne died really knows, one of a few, what it has been like for me. I had tearful moments with Gary and David, solemn sharing with Tara and Shelley as with Dave. We all confronted the reality of your death once more.

The weather was sunny, the gardens beautiful and Alice pointed out, as usual, the lilac trees we presented to them as a house gift. I had a few bites of a really fat hot dog "special" for you but as you know really preferred the rare hamburger that Bill grilled especially for me.

You have been in our thoughts and hearts every day not just this Father's Day weekend. I learned that both Tara and her doctor believe that her recent colitis 'flare up' was related to stress, perhaps her grief for you, as you had been a loving "father" to her.

Shelley is considering leaving her job and has not yet come to some conclusion. She told Gary that if you were alive you would have been able to help her with her decision. Did you not help me, Linda and countless others in listening to a professional dilemma and helped us sort out the issues in order to go forward?

I love you, Harriet

June 19

Dear Jerry,

And so it is over! Father's Day, our first since you died! There was much anticipation, both conscious and not. The days before and after have been filled with emotional phone calls, lots of tears but you can continue to be proud of your sons. They are courageous, sensitive, compassionate, loving to me and their wives and children and look to you as their hero and role model.

Father's Day was sad. But sad is not bad! Yes, it hurts me to listen to my child crying and yet I know that is all I can do. I will continue to listen to each one knowing full well that is what will continue to heal us. And I will cry with them as they listen to me.

The golf tournament ended sadly for Phil Mickelson who had it in his hands and then on the 18th hole reverted to an old negative pattern. It was sad, too, for Tiger Woods who didn't make the cut having returned only nine weeks since his dad's death. How many countless others were saddened by Fathers' Day this year?

Death changes so much and yet so much rarely changes.

Sad as it was, we smiled, played with the children, ate, drank, laughed, and felt alive because we are alive and have so much to be grateful for. I think of you every day—not just on Father's Day.

I love you, Harriet

June 20 (11 p.m.)

Dear Jerry,

The Galperns stayed here last night and Dave and I took time for sharing while sitting on the porch.

He said of you, "As long as one heart beats in one of the grand-children," you "will remain alive."

He told me he had wanted to say that at the unveiling but couldn't. He also spoke of how you are with him daily and just yesterday he brought along the cashew logo golf balls I gave him so he could have you close when on the golf course. He even explained that to his foursome when they inquired about the unusual logo. Guess what? Maybe you helped them win with their low gross that day.

This morning the three of us sat outside eating breakfast when we heard the pitter-patter of little feet on the porch roof. Not since last September during Shiva week did I see or hear the mourning doves on the roof. It certainly felt like you wanted to be with us.

Today Gary came by on his way to the cemetery to check out the Zen garden. He loved the garden, as did Louise and David. We had some lunch together and conversation, of course, all in our favorite room, the porch. There were words, tears and silence as well. It was precious time together. How grateful I am for every moment shared with people I love and who love me.

Josh wrote a letter from camp comparing the white water rafting he did with us a couple of years ago, to his recent experience in camp as "more fun..." How sweet is that! He's waterskiing and loves it and wants to do it with me one day. Of course I had told him how we used to love to water ski during the years of our dating and early years of our marriage. Oh, if you could only be sharing these moments with us. I hope you do see it all.

I love you, Harriet

June 26 (7 a.m.)

Dear Jerry,

A week has gone by but it's not like I haven't been thinking about you or talking about you or missing you.

I have four private clients on Tuesday after a full day at the hospice office and when I finish the best thing for me is to go to sleep. I did that. I'm taking care of myself.

Wednesday was a beautiful day in every respect. I had invited Lee and Jim to play golf so after working in the morning we met at 2:00. (I fit in a 45minute bike ride beforehand.) The weather was ideal, sunny in the 80's, with very little humidity. We all hit the ball well, laughed, complimented each other and were so relaxed. Then we went back to our house so they could see the garden, have drinks and dinner that I had prepared. They didn't leave until 10 and we all acknowledged it was a special time.

As Lee said, "the way we had when it was the four of us."

We talked about you and Kathleen and the fact that a year was coming up since both deaths. We reminisced about how we each heard about your deaths. I had forgotten that you and I had a date to see Lee and Jim on Wednesday night, the day after you died. We also spoke of new life, Jake Thomas Cunningham, Kevin and Lorie's first child. I loved hearing Lee's phone message the next day and listened to it repeatedly taking in the love, gratitude and joy in her voice reflecting on our special day, our unique relationship as well as the sadness we all are feeling missing you. By the way Jim proudly showed me he was wearing your watch that I had given him back in December.

Speaking of showing, Shelley always wears the bracelet I bought for her when at the convention in Florida. It is so pretty on her and she is so thoughtful that way knowing it reminds me of attending my last nut convention and playing in the Jerry Vogel Memorial Golf Tournament.

Gary and Shelley went to London for the weekend and Allie and Grant stayed with me. There were several references to you and you should have seen as you probably did, Allie's bewildered look on her face when she spotted your photo as the screensaver on my computer desktop.

Craig and Amy continue to have quality time while the boys are away in camp for a month. I'm happy for them, knowing how important that is for a marriage.

Ed is going through some cardiac testing these days but Craig doesn't think it's a major concern. Prayers certainly won't hurt.

I will stop writing you now. I want to exercise before work.

I love you, Harriet

June 30 (11 p.m.)

Dear Jerry,

Wednesday was a healing day. I met my friend Susann for lunch and we talked about our two Jerry's who have died and reminisced about our hospice trip to Russia soon after her husband's death many years ago.

Afterwards, I spontaneously went to the cemetery and noticed just a quiet sadness—no tears—when at your grave. I then went to our parents' graves and learned quickly that "perpetual care" means once a year cutting the shrubs. I guess I will have to put a pair of work gloves, shears and a garbage bag into my car trunk and do what my parents used to do; periodically go to the cemetery and clean up the graves.

A deep massage that night, completed a healing day for me.

Here it is Friday night and I am sitting on your side of the guest bed in Louise and Dave's house in Sheffield. I came up this morning. It was a spontaneous decision as their plans had changed and I had no plans for Friday and Saturday. The weather is spectacular after weeks of rain. We took in a movie and now I'm tired and need to go to sleep. It feels so good to be here with them.

I love you, Harriet

July 1 (11 p.m.)

Dear Jerry,

Life goes on! Golf, visits, parties and you're here only in spirit, memories and reflections. Early in the morning I took a walk remembering when you and I used to walk along Hickey Hill Road. Then I played golf with Louise and David and silently thanked you for introducing me to the game when we were dating. Dan and Cori visited and I wished you were here to see them, her pregnant belly and their love and excitement awaiting the birth of their first child. Elaine and Steve came by too and it would have been more complete if you were sitting with us on the porch. As Elaine was leaving she asked me to tell her when I feel ready to meet someone. Louise also shared they have had conversations with Phoebe and Ed and they agreed they would welcome me with someone.

Tonight I joined Louise and David at a party where I was introduced as Harriet, not of Harriet and Jerry. I was very aware of the difference. Yet, I met some interesting people and had great conversations and a good time. I am finding myself once again enjoying classical music and jazz again, the music I loved before you died, no longer needing to hear nostalgic love songs or oldies.

Times are changing. I feel lighter. I have more energy. I'm thinking of my future, the prospect of dating but I will always love you and our life together.

I love you, Harriet

July 3

Dear Jerry,

I drove back from the Berkshires yesterday in order to play in the July 4 tournament with Barry. Jane is recuperating from back surgery so I was his partner. Helene and Warren were in our "six some". What memories I have of this annual event at NSCC, everyone in red, white and blue, skits, costumes, hot weather, long rounds. I missed the jokes when we had played with our old group but Barry was so easy to play with and he hit some fantastic shots. When I gave him a golf watch from your memorial golf tournament after our round he showed me that his watch wasn't working. No accidents I say. I have one more watch left. That one I will keep for myself.

When returning from the Berkshires I noticed no phone messages on the answering machine. While it was unusual, it told me things are back to normal for the most part. I'm pleased that the boys and their families have rich full lives. It reminds me of how life was before you died and it makes it easier for me to go about my life too. As much as I love being with them, I need my peers, my activities, and my space to be me. You always did that for me giving me the room to grow and flourish. I'm forever grateful to you and for our long rich life together.

I love you, Harriet

July 6 (7 a.m.)

Dear Jerry,

I got back from NYC last night after seeing an Off, Off Broadway show with Ruth and Bayla about grief, counseling and relationships, perfect for the three of us, to listen to six new phone messages. And Tuesday night after coming back from viewing the fireworks with Phoebe and Ed at his cousins' Manhattan rooftop there were seven messages. While that seems like a lot I feel different now. I call it "lighter." I also noticed my last visit to the cemetery was less emotional, outwardly. It was a solemn visit with my being quiet and reading the words inscribed on the footstone and touching it lovingly. I have observed I have more energy. For example, after three days of outdoor sports and activities, and lots of driving, I worked in the hospice office from 9-5, counseling on the phone and in person, did administrative work and prepared for my "Coping With The High Holy Days After the Death of a Loved One" Workshop, then saw a private client at home and went to yoga never feeling any tiredness. That was most unusual! I used to need a nap before a night yoga session.

Helene and Warren stopped by after class to see the Zen garden and they too loved it. All the rain we have been having has helped the new plantings, especially the bamboo. I can hardly see the neighbors. (You know which yard I am talking about.)

I'm taking care of more household things; black topped the driveway, ordered screen repair for the porch, had the gutters cleaned and fixed. You would be proud of me but then again you always were. My newest challenge is to install my new printer. I don't mean plugging it in after removing it from the box. I have to try one more time before asking for help. I already had "two fatal errors." I also decided to buy a new wet/dry vacuum. I can't remember the last time you bought one but it was needed! Next I will need to look for a new TV for the den. As I continue to keep the house going I am grateful I have the health, awareness, strength, serenity, support and money to do all I'm doing as I navigate the "Pitch of Grief", the title to a movie I have shown in my bereavement groups.

Glad I was home yesterday morning to receive a phone call offering me an earlier appointment with the medium Glenn Dove for Saturday at 11 instead of my original one for July 19 the day before I am leaving for Israel. I'm ready I believe to connect with you. I hope you are ready to connect with me.

I love you, Harriet

July 8 (11:30 p.m.)

Dear Jerry,

What a night! What a day! Let me start with tonight, the 100th Anniversary of the Association of Food Industries, your association, at the Roosevelt Hotel in New York City. Ed arranged for me to join him and Enid by private car. Limos are fun. It was an overwhelming tribute to those who had been part of the association since its inception. There were films running at the cocktail hour and more after dinner as well as photo albums displayed on tables for all to peruse. You were in many photos and films. I loved the one of us dancing. Your name was mentioned in speeches and viewed upon a large screen for all to see. Many people came up to me to tell me how happy they were to see me and how much you are missed in the industry. It was wonderful for me, not sad, to hear these precious words and feelings shared by so many. It reminded me of my experience in Florida back in January at the PTNPA. I never minded that you often were talking business at these social events. I always loved being Jerry's wife at all business dinners and conventions. I guess I just loved being Jerry's wife.

This morning I had a blast "listening" to you. Well, I mean I visited a medium, someone who has the ability to channel the spirits of dead people. I know this is something you never quite believed in and even questioned whether there was an afterlife. The funny part was that one of the things he said about you was that you weren't a believer before your death and you still weren't sure about it now. I laughed out loud. A few tears were shed during the session but more laughs—it was so you—the smile, your dry sense of humor, the conversation, the caring and love, the gentleness, very affirming and I will be looking for a sign as you assured me that you will accompany us to Israel.

I was so energized after that I continued with my plan to go for a bike ride from Cedar Creek Park in Wantagh to Jones Beach. I had the bike on the bike rack and was already dressed in my cycling clothes. Remember when we took our boys on this ride when they were young? I rode the route twice and I felt so alive. I loved that it ended at Jones Beach, reminding me of all our beach days spent on LI and in the Caribbean, the BVI's, Bermuda, the Bahamas, Hawaii, Israel, France, Maine and Nantucket. It was a wonderful day and I look forward to another tomorrow. It starts in two minutes.

I love you, Harriet

July 13/14 (midnight)

Dear Jerry,

This has been a tumultuous week. The weather went from beautifully perfect summer days to torrential rain, with wicked rainstorms and even tornadoes ripping through parts of Westchester and Connecticut.

A small-scale border event involving an abducted soldier in Gaza has escalated today with Arabs killing and abducting soldiers on the Lebanon border as well. Israel has now retaliated by bombing Beirut Airport and Hamas hideouts. Haifa and Safed had rockets fired on them today. We are days away from leaving for Israel for the long awaited Bar Mitzvah trip and there is a strong possibility we may not go.

Monday and Tuesday was the start of new widow/widowers/partners support groups and they went well. Glad to be doing my work.

Phoebe and Ed were here tonight and we shared wine and food, laughter and tears, words and letters, books and memories. And I got a little help with the new printer from Ed. And as usual we talked about you. I shared about my session with the medium Glenn Dove. Ed is awaiting a medical report from a specialist and that was touched on too.

There were many connections this week by phone with people I seldom hear from. I guess that may be because it is almost 11 months since you died. I always helped mourners recognize that 3, 6, 9 and 11 months are trigger times in the first year grief cycle, usually bringing more intense grief reactions. There's no scientific explanation that I know of but it happens.

Today is the first anniversary of Kathleen's death. I can remember you sitting on your side of the bed having answered the early morning call from Lee and Jim telling us that their daughter Kathleen had died suddenly. That call was a year ago. I miss you so much as they miss her. Losing a child is so devastating. Sometimes I wonder how bereaved parents get through each day. And yet I know on some level because the many bereaved parents I have counseled have taught me that healing is possible but it takes acknowledging the reality, feeling the emotions of grief and being realistic about the many months and years it may take to feel a "new normal".

I love you, Harriet

July 14 (11:30 p.m.)

Dear Jerry,

Shabbat Shalom! Went to services with Lois and Stu and then went out for dinner. Not surprising but we talked about you and it is clear you are loved and dearly missed by them too. I had a lovely evening with them. Long time friendships are so special.

I had a surprise lunch guest today; David. Ironically I was at home when he called to say he would be in the area and believe it or not he ate the quick lunch I had prepared. I know I have been the butt of many jokes by the boys about my food not withstanding the fact that on the night you died I had served a vegetarian dinner. We sat at the bistro table in the Zen garden and I had acknowledged once more that it was his idea to create this garden and I love it so. We talked as the bees hummed about the flowering shrubs.

The new TV was delivered today but it will have to be installed and the space redone to accommodate the size. Fear not. I will take care of that as well.

Spoke with Craig and Brian today about Israel and the latest in the fight for peace. It's still too early to decide if we are going on Wednesday. You did say through Glenn Dove that you would come with us and give me a sign. Do I take that as a fact that we will be traveling on the 19th? I hope so. Good night.

I love you, Harriet

July 16 (10:30 p.m.)

Dear Jerry,

Craig and Amy have made a final decision to cancel, as the war in Israel is more intense. Needless to say I feel very disappointed but recognize the prudent decision. My guess is you would have made the same decision but only earlier. It is not only sad for me but I think of all the preparation Josh had done for his Bar Mitzvah ceremony in Israel as well as Craig and Amy in planning the trip.

I spent the day at the beach with David, Tara and the girls and it was a beautiful and hot day and it reminded me of Israel in July 1980, our first trip there with the family. I was hoping to rekindle that memory this week in Tel Aviv.

Ed came by yesterday and was so helpful in setting up the controls for the new TV, VCR and DVD. Wish you could enjoy it all with me.

It's your dad's yahrzeit so I will go downstairs and light a candle in his memory and remember him with love. Even though you told me he was a stern father and stubborn man I knew him as a sweet and doting father in law who loved to make us laugh with a caper or two. He was also a fine boater and fisherman. You may not remember this but he taught me golf etiquette and the simple way to place a ball on a tee. Wish you were here with me to light the candle and say the prayer together.

I love you, Harriet

July 19 (11 p.m.)

Dear Jerry,

We would have been on an El Al flight to Israel if it weren't
for major military conflicts on the Lebanon and Gaza borders.
Instead, I picked up Josh and Matthew as they flew in today
on their own. They already had the tickets to New York. After
settling in, Matthew and I went food shopping (he loves the su-
permarket) and then we all drove to Jones Beach for miniature
golf and a snack dinner. Had some laughs and fun and I was reminded of the time you and I took Yavin and Matan there after
they flew in with their parents from Israel years ago. We passed
the dance area where music was playing and many people were
enjoying ballroom dancing under the stars. Memories flooded
back and I told the boys about how you and I had loved to
dance. I believe our last dance together was celebrating Louise
and David's anniversary at that fabulous outdoor party at their
country home.

This morning I had a very special visit with Alice. I confronted her about her saying she didn't have time to see me even
though I had learned she and Bill were on LI from Monday
through this evening. In that phone call from me she finally
agreed to meet for about 30 minutes over breakfast. It ended
up for almost 3 hours. We had not had this quality of time since
you died. I believed she and Bill had been avoiding me as I am
a reminder of you and your death. We sat on the porch and she
cried and shared and I sat and listened. You were here for her
always, she said. You were her rock, she admitted. And during
this year, I believe they didn't know how to process their grief

for you. I had realized a while ago that you had given so much to them through the years until your death. Nevertheless it didn't lessen my feelings of having been abandoned by them. I had always tried to help my clients understand there sometimes are secondary losses we experience after the death of a loved one. For me that's what I had to process and it wasn't easy. I hope we can heal this relationship. By the end of the visit I told Alice I felt like I had 26 years ago when she and I first sat on chairs in the ocean at Nassau Beach talking and connecting. For me sad is not bad but it has to be shared.

I'm tired. This morning was highly emotional. The afternoon was pretty physical. If you were here I wouldn't have had to go through all this.

I love you, Harriet

July 23 (8 a.m.)

Dear Jerry,

Hardly have a minute to write as I have been very busy. Thursday I took the boys kayaking as planned in the same waters where you and I had gone with Helene and Warren one time. Just about everything I do reminds me of you. We took three singles with Matthew requesting his own. We had some adventure! Even though he had kayaked solo before in camp he never had to sustain 2 1/2 hours with wind, current and torrential rain in his face. It wasn't that way when we took off but the weather changed and we had to fight those conditions coming back. We laughed a lot and could hardly keep our eyes open because of the pelting raindrops but in the end we saw it as fun.

When we returned home I had intended to take a well needed nap but Josh thought he would like to put together the arbor I had bought for the garden. Neither handyman ever called back so I was grateful for his offer. Of course I helped him and lo and behold it is complete. He even began sealing it. Then it was time to take warm showers and get some dinner. We tried a new restaurant with beautiful décor and delicious food, each boy trying new dishes, sauces and flavors. They were very "courageous". The ice cream store next door was a natural stop for dessert. They had been there before with you they remembered. They talked about you. We missed you. We were sad, but sad is not bad.

After borrowing Phoebe and Ed's car, Matthew and I picked Craig and Amy up at JFK. When I returned the car I happily learned that Ed's test results were ok just as Craig had suggested. That's a relief.

Friday while I saw a private client, Craig, Amy and Josh went to the cemetary. Matthew had visited there earlier that day with David prior to going to his printing plant. The six of us met together at the house. After lunch Tara and the girls came by on their way out to visit with friends in Sag Harbor and with their need for only one car David lent us his (your car) so we could drive to the city to see the "Bodies Exhibit", a realistic display of all parts and systems of the human body. It was well done and educational and I think everyone but Matthew enjoyed it. Rain hindered us from really enjoying the South Street Seaport in its entirety.

Saturday the weather forecast was still calling for storms so after a great bike ride with Josh, I fixed the fountain. I'm always cleaning it from residue but it's worth it. I love the sound of flowing water in the garden. That's healing too.

Matthew did more staining of the arbor. Amy and Matthew then headed to the city by train to buy jewelry for her business and Craig, Josh and I drove in to take a tour of the UN, very timely with respect to the current Mid East crisis. We all connected as planned and drove to Connecticut to visit with Gary and Shelley and the kids. We saw their new house, his new sports car, played and had dinner together. All of that was mixed with conversation and laughter and missing you.

You can imagine how exhausted I must have been. After the hour's drive home I slept for 9 hours thankfully. Weather is still not looking hopeful so I am not sure we will be going on Gary's boat today as planned.

I love you, Harriet

July 23 (10:30 p.m.)

Dear Jerry,

While Craig, Amy and Josh drove back to Connecticut to go boating (Matthew slept over) I chose to remain home for several reasons. The main reason was to give them all time together without me. I clearly remember the difference when we as a family were with or without our parents. Each experience is important. I benefitted too from that decision.

I had a chance to watch the final 5 holes of the British Open with Tiger Woods winning, and the ensuing emotion as he articulated publicly the reason for all the tears—his love for and missing his dad. Runner up Chris DeMarco was grieving for his mother who had died of a heart attack July 4. I sat. I watched. I cried. I cried for them, for me, and for our sons. Remember; sad is not bad.

Craig and his family returned to LI and David and his family came from out east and together with your sister we all had Eddie's pizza for dinner, this time on our porch. It was another great time together but you weren't here to enjoy it, as you would have. Being in Israel at this time would have been better too.

I love you, Harriet

July 27 (11 p.m.)

Dear Jerry,

Even though I trust that you know everything I still have the need to write to you.

A recap of the week: Craig, Amy and the boys left at 6:30 a.m. Monday for a vacation in Colorado in lieu of Israel. I went to work as usual Monday and Tuesday.

Wednesday morning I dreamt about you just as I was waking at 7, the time I was to talk to Marcia to confirm our walking time. I recalled the dream and described it to Marcia. Now it is difficult to bring the details back. I know you were happy to see me but you were eating sweets (perhaps chocolates) and I told you your blood sugar was high. There were other people but the details are so blurry. I wish I could remember the rest. But it always feels soothing to dream of you.

Yesterday was one year since Gene died so Marcia and I walked for fifty minutes and talked about how we had been in a cocoon this first year, surrounded by family and friends and doing familiar activities in familiar places. She is breaking out of her cocoon by going on a trip to China. Even though she invited me to join her, that destination no longer holds the same interest for me since I cancelled our trip after your death.

I have been thinking about what Marcia said of being in a cocoon. It's time to try things on our own like emerging butterflies. I always wanted to take a bike tour, different than when you and I took our bikes to Nantucket and the Outer Banks or when Jane and I biked on our own in Holland. Last night I went on the Internet and checked on bike tours up and down the east coast. I called this morning and there is available room with a company called Sojourn. Tonight I confirmed and I will leave September 3 for a bike trip to Martha's Vineyard and Nantucket. Going back to Nantucket will trigger many memories for me of when you and I went with only two bicycles and two duffle bags, but I will handle it. I look forward to the beaches, water views, cycling and hopefully warm weather. Labor Day weekend last year was very different. I stayed in my home and hundreds came by to pay their respects as part of the Shiva week. This year I will go out and explore new territory, meet new people and rediscover a memorable island by myself, an antidote to what some experience as the harder second year. I am even thinking of visiting with one or two people I know who live in the Boston area and tag that on to the bike trip. I am exhilarated by these plans; an amazing contrast to the fatigue I felt Monday and Tuesday when I almost fell asleep at the staff support meeting.

Tonight I asked Ed to have dinner with me since Phoebe flew down to Florida to bring their granddaughter Sammy up for a week. For a long time I have wanted to go to Café Picasso on a Thursday night because they have a psychic every week. This was Ed's first experience with a psychic. He's a real skeptic in this area but I found what she shared to be right on target. I learned from her, as if I didn't know it, that you and I are very connected. You are with my dad and having fun. You want me to be happy and I could have guessed that too. You want me to live my life. I liked hearing that. Knowing Ed wouldn't let me pay for dinner I paid for our sessions with the psychic. Of course, I think he's still a non-believer.

Lots of grief work for me these last few weeks; triggers, emotions, challenges and disappointment. But it's changing...my grief, that is. That's the one thing I could always guarantee my clients. Grief changes. I learned that from a bereaved mother who joined a support group for bereaved parents of adult children years ago. She introduced herself by saying this was the second adult child that had died, both of AIDS.

When another parent asked her how did she cope after the first death she replied, "It changes."

I have learned so much from my clients. "You are the expert," I used to say. "You are the one going through the grief."

Now it's my turn. Now I'm the expert. I know sad is not bad.

I love you, Harriet

July 31 (10:00 a.m.)

Dear Jerry,

The weather is perfect with clear blue skies, warm temperatures with a slight breeze. I had a great bike ride this morning and was at the doctor's for my checkup: all ok! Marty joined me for services at Temple and then we went out for dinner. We talked about you, Marilyn, his journey, mine, his girlfriend and how they had met, his concerns, his hopes, my concerns and my hopes and then asked if I would want to sail with him and his children tomorrow. Well you know it didn't take me two seconds to jump at the opportunity. Marty borrowed a friend's J 29 on which he races on Thirsty Thursdays. He offered and I accepted to be at the tiller most of the time. I loved the wind in my face, the sound of the boat moving through the water towards the Throg's Neck Bridge, the action, the company and the familiar and beautiful surroundings of Manhasset Bay. Oh how many wonderful sails we did share on Long Island Sound on our sailboat, "Relections".

At Shabbat services I met Marcia's family as they were there for Gene's yahrzeit. It was important for me to support her at this year anniversary. She agreed to walk with me on August 30 as I did with her last week.

I have asked Sue to go to dinner with me after services the night of your yahrzeit and I was thinking of going to Galleria Restaurant as a nostalgic memory of your many times dining there both for business and pleasure. Maybe the boys will come too.

Sunday was beautiful too. I spent time with Linda at her house, then played 9 boles of golf and rejoined her for a movie in the evening. I'm blessed with good friends. I am blessed with a good life. Thank you again.

I love you, Harriet

July 31 (1:30 p.m.)

Dear Jerry,

How could I forget to tell you that now I am using your golf bag and humongous woods. I realized Friday I was using an old style bag and the new ones are lighter and better for the caddies. So I changed to your lightweight navy golf bag. Then I looked at your clubs just hanging out in the basement and compared them to mine for height and weight, and after finding little difference I gave them a try on Friday. They were working well yesterday.

I know you always joked when you or someone else bought a new club saying, "There is a set number of good shots in each new club."

I wonder how many are left in yours? For me they are such a great connection to you.

P.S. I began work today on creating memory books for each of the boys and their families. Tell you more as I progress.

I love you, Harriet

YAHRZEIT

August 2 (8 a.m.)

Dear Jerry,

Yesterday, August 1 was a day of connecting to you on so many levels.

Spoke to Gary in the morning and he made mention of the date August 1. It will be one year August 30, this month, last year. It seems like yesterday.

"Can't believe it is a year," said Gary.

Gary and I spoke about Wednesday, August 30 and Friday, September 1 when your name will be read from the pulpit and that that was the actual date of your funeral last year. Similar comments came from Craig and David later in the day.

David and I met spontaneously for lunch. He was on his way

from his Freeport plant to NYC and I was at the hospice office and free at lunchtime. He picked me up in "your car". It's still your car in my eyes even though it never seemed to fit your style. Maybe that's why it doesn't trigger me when I see David driving it. I loved and associated you with the Jaguars that you drove since 1980. As we left the parking lot, 3000 Marcus was in view and of course that is where your office was for so many years. Just then David said to me, "It's no accident that we're together today without prior planning," and asked me if I knew what he meant. Of course it was the date August 1.

He shared how he was sad in the morning and Tara said, "Don't be sad."

He knew she meant, "I hope you're not sad," but he took it as a teachable moment for her and said, "I can be sad and so can you."

How beautiful is that! It is so important to acknowledge the reality of death in our lives and embrace the emotions and feelings that accompany the grief. I know through my personal and professional experience that that is what helps heal us.

All our Marriage Encounter experience has certainly paid off as our boys, I mean men, seem to have learned to communicate in healthy, responsible ways, by sharing their feelings.

I told David a little about my psychic visit with you through Glenn Dove and I believe he too will choose to go one day. I am not so sure about Craig and Gary who are more cynical.

I called Craig for nothing more than to continue talking about the connection with August 1. Josh answered and told me of his new passion, riding a racing bike, and he is now tall enough to be using yours, the one I shipped down originally for Craig. When he visited me this summer he rode a road bike for the first time and liked it. He said your bike is a perfect size and he's hoping to get cycling shorts, a mirror for his helmet and bike gloves too. Craig got on the phone and while today's date had not triggered him he too can't believe it will be one year.

You know how much I love to buy and send greeting cards especially unique ones. Years ago I came across a card that I have kept to remind me to send this very message to friends and family who are approaching the one-year mark of their losses. It reads, "In some ways a year seems like forever and in others it feels like yesterday." The inside continues with, "On this anniversary you are in our hearts." And you are in ours, Jerry.

Dr. Sussman left a voice message for Craig while they were away and Craig returned the call just today, August 1. It was just another follow up call he said because he thinks of the family and you a lot. Thanks to him and your dedicated approach to lead a healthy life, you did survive and lived fully for another 17 years after the first heart attack. For that I am grateful.

In speaking with Stu last night, when he asked how the boys and I were doing, I was proud to answer, "We are so honest and supportive of one another," and it is true.

Gary and David, Craig and Gary, David and Craig, Craig and

Gary…their calls, visits and with their mom too…every one of us…We really did raise three special men. I'm so proud to have been your partner in so many aspects of life – lovers, friends, parents, and in sports too.

The tears are falling as I'm writing this but I'm ready to take a bike ride by myself. That's what I need to do to change my mood. It's very hot out and it reminds me of the record break-ing heat during the summer of 1988 when you had your first heart attack—and 1980 when we traveled as a family to Israel for the first time; happy and sad memories all rolled into one. But I also try to remember sad is not bad.

I love you, Harriet

August 7 (8 a.m.)

Dear Jerry,

You would have loved this past weekend. I drove up to Louise and David Saturday afternoon for an impromptu getaway. The drive up was spectacular as everything was lush and green and the skies were clear. Saturday afternoon I sat looking at the butterflies hovering over the beautifully colored flowers in Louise's garden. We went to Tanglewood Saturday night and even though the music was Mahler sitting on the lawn under the starry sky was dreamy. You know I prefer that to sitting in-side. Louise stayed there with me while David sat in the shed. See, you could have had the other seat in the shed if you liked. Sunday morning we all slept late and after I did yoga on the lawn we had a leisurely breakfast with Michael and Danielle, Dan's friends, who were guests here too as they were checking the progress of the construction of their new home. We talked and laughed and recalled this weekend here last year, the anniversary of the memorable outdoor party hosted by Louise and David. I shared how that was our last dance. They remembered sitting at the same table as our children watching us dance. I think we were the only ones on the dance floor at one time but that wasn't unusual for us. I so loved to be in your arms and feel you close to me. I also liked how we would wonder why we would get compliments about our dancing when we were only doing "our thing". We also remembered the delicious lobsters that were served and cracked for us but most importantly that the party was then and not the following November in Florida, the actual anniversary month of the Galperns. If it were held in November there would have been one less guest. You.

Then the three of us went to play golf and I played out of Louise's bag again. I was hitting her driver and hybrids pretty well. Last night Louise entertained in her inimitable way, inviting Jane and Alan over for steaks and corn. I loved the spontaneity of the weekend and the loving people who surrounded and nurtured me.

Last week I took care of myself in some very positive ways – a massage, a visit to my professional supervisor, a one woman show that was great, services Friday night followed by dinner with Abby, a fascinating, accomplished and warm woman, and a two hour bike ride with Janie who wanted a "tune up ride" before her trip to Latvia.

I'm so fortunate. My life is full. But I miss you Jer.

I love you, Harriet

August 11 (10 p.m.)

Dear Jerry,

Tonight I treated myself—perhaps a weird way to say it. I took myself to a movie called "Boynton Beach Club." The reviews I read suggested this would be good to see professionally, as it is the story of a bereavement group of widows and widowers in Florida. I also remember laughing a lot when I saw the coming attractions. I thought of three people I would want to see it with so I first asked your sister but she was too busy getting ready to go away. I thought I would ask Marcia to join me but she was going on her first date. Good for her! I would have asked Lorraine but she flew to Seattle last night to visit Cathy and then on to Alaska.

I chose to see it alone at North Shore Towers. I was happy not to have met anyone in the theater who I knew from bereavement groups I had facilitated in the past. I wanted to be anonymous. However, I did meet "Harriet the grieving widow." I thought the movie was well done and realistic about the grief issues, but the dating process was so new to me, as it was to the characters in the story. I laughed a lot and then I cried a lot when "Earth Angel" was played at a 50's theme New Year's Eve party during one of the closing scenes. It brought it all back to me—memories of dating you in the 50's. Then I looked into the future watching three people dating for their first time in thirty five to forty years with aging bodies, teenage feelings, nudity and intimacy with a new person—and experiencing new life again. Even though they were from our time, married in the 60's they all except for one couple looked so old to me. I was able to relate to one woman, though, as she was thin, energetic and athletic. She and her boyfriend looked much younger but I guess that was realistic too. There is no timetable for death and none for reentering the "couples" world. It was also a bit sad for me as death is occurring more frequently at my age.

To think the only reason I would consider dating is because you have died! That is another reality check and trigger for tears. They came, the tears. But sad is not bad, I remind myself.

Last night I was looking through our old photos, of dating you and of my Sweet 16 surprise party. I also was rereading some of the many letters I wrote you when you were in the army. You know, the ones I wrote using purple ink, the ones that survived the flooded basement but were often illegible in parts. Then I reread the eulogies given at your funeral. I'm preparing books of memory for each family and choosing significant photos and writings to be included—all triggers for tears and healing. I found the perfect saying for the first page. Samuel Friedman, in *Who She Was* wrote "When you are sorrowful look again in your heart...see that in truth you are weeping for that which has been your delight."

It was good for me to take so much time to go through old things and be by myself—especially this month leading up to the year anniversary.

Spent a couple of hours (don't tell my office) with Helene, first in her new apartment to see the progress, and then lunch in my garden. Time to talk and be together. I needed it. I am so lucky to have friends who continue to be there for me and have been since the day you died.

Time well spent!

I love you, Harriet

August 11 (11 p.m.)

Dear Jerry,

Can you believe "services by the sea"? Well, by the bay anyway. Bernadette invited me to join her and her congregation for outdoor Shabbat Services at Cold Spring Harbor. It sounded like a great idea and when Helene asked if I were going to services, since Warren was away I suggested she join us. Prior to services and a setting sun the three of us had dinner outdoors in a nearby restaurant. The sky was spectacular.

I know you would have said, "If I had my paints I could paint now."

You never did paint except house painting. Maybe now you are creating scenes like I saw tonight. Unforgettable! And so was my golf today having been invited as a guest to play Sands

Point. What a beautiful tract, with two of the holes overlooking Hempstead Harbor. It was a number 10 day, weather wise and I was hitting your clubs so well, including your old putter. I am having the grips changed with leather and they will be made narrower for me as well.

I love you, Harriet

August 13 (8:30 a.m.)

Dear Jerry,

I woke up alone in a charming small bedroom at Shelly and Mark's country home, the same one I used last year soon after your death. I'm visiting this weekend along with Phoebe and Ed. Of course you remember this was a plan for last summer but we had to cancel the last minute when Helen died. It was a nostalgic ride up Route 17 again and this time Ed shared some of his memories of this area. Phoebe sat in the back as she is healing a sprained ankle.

Mark and Ed fished and "the girls" headed to a local fair in town. Later Mark served green apple martinis and we ate a yummy dinner. Conversation was about how Mark and Shelly met through Internet dating; the pros, cons, and new relationships. I took it all in as this may be my choice in the future. Of course it would be easier if you sent someone my way. Could it be that last night's dream was connected to that conversation? In the dream I was with a faceless "someone", holding hands, and then our bodies were lying together and in leaving "he" said, "take it slow." I'll keep that in mind. Shelly had said she dated two years before meeting Mark. Phoebe had said that I would have trouble not comparing people to you. All of that is true. You have set a very high standard with your youthful, energetic, soft-spoken, considerate and loving qualities.

Fortunately you and I had conversations about the "what if's?" What if I died first; what if you died first? We were realistic and planned for the inevitable. We purchased cemetery plots. We presented at Marriage Encounter on the theme of death and dying at least twice. We spoke of my work in hospice. We experienced deaths of family and close friends. We gave each other permission to find a new partner when the time came.

One of the most poignant writings I received this past year was one that I laminated and tucked into a photo frame holding a favorite photo of us together. It reads, "And if I go while you're still here…know that I live on, vibrating to a different measure—behind a thin veil you cannot see through. You will not see me, so you must have faith. I wait for the time when we will soar together again, both aware of each other. Until then, live your life to its fullest. And when you need me, just whisper my name in your heart… I will be there."

I love you, Harriet

August 16 (11:30 p.m.)

Dear Jerry,

I finished packing for my trip to see Kris and Dave in Grand Rapids. It would have been a snap a few weeks ago, one small carry-on, but a few weeks ago a major plot to blow up a plane with liquid chemicals has changed carry-on to no creams or liquids. Since I had to check my small "carry-on" I decided to also bring your golf clubs and bag as I hope to play with Dave. That way I'll feel like I'm bringing you along. I also have a photo of you for him, at his request.

Tonight was a Marriage Encounter meeting at Lois and Stu's home. It was strange that even though it was a perfect evening for an outdoor meeting, they held it indoors. Lois said she thinks Stu consciously suggested meeting indoors so it wouldn't be a trigger for me, a reminder of the meeting there last summer just one week before you died. During the time when we write a love letter to our spouse, I chose to go outdoors and reflect on that memorable meeting one year ago in that very garden. It was our last meeting together and I flipped through my book and reread the letters I had written to you since August 2005. I took advantage of the time and place to revisit these memories and surprisingly it was not sad for me.

I found the "perfect" card and bought six copies, which will hold a letter I have written to each grandchild for your one-year anniversary. The outer page reads "Love is eternal" and inside the message continues, "In your sorrow may you find comfort from the memories woven from good times." I wrote about a unique memory or two that I hope each child will cherish about you.

In Josh's I referred to the time you and he spent together just weeks before you died. As our oldest grandchild I asked that he speak about you and your endearing qualities to his younger brother and cousins.

To Matthew I wrote how he was named after your father, his great grandfather Milton, having been given the same Hebrew name, Moshe. He enjoyed asking you, "Did you check your sugar yet?" I reminded him that he was always there to help you check your blood sugar when you were together.

In Jessie's letter I wrote that when you saw her, our first grand daughter, through the nursery windows, "He admired how pretty and delicate you were - a real girl. He always complimented you in your pretty dresses and skirts."

I wrote to Allie about her following us down to the car when we were leaving and after you lowered the car window she had been lifted by Gary and gave you a final kiss. Your response was, "That was worth the trip." And I added, "You were a blessing in his life."

To Riley I wrote, "You were Grandpa's little girl and he was Grandpa Cashew to you." I added, "I will always remember that every time you and I spoke on the telephone you had always asked, 'Where's Grandpa?' You were only two when he died and you continued to ask that question both on the phone and when you visited in our home." And I always answered with the words, 'He died.' knowing that even with young children we must use the word 'died' and not some euphemism.

In Grant's letter I referred to how he greeted you at the door with his exuberant voice, "Gran Pa!" which spoke of his love for you even though he was not yet two. I added, "You also showed him how well you were hitting the golf ball in your backyard."

I ended all their letters with, "Know that Grandpa is always with you and will love and protect you as you grow. Love, Nanny August 30, 2006"

It's always so sad for me to think of how cheated they are of your presence in their lives. They are so young. I was the fortunate one—fifty years together.

Today I made copies of photos from early childhood through to your last birthday celebrations in Florida and New York. Next week I will be collating these books as a tangible tribute to who you were.

I love you and wish you were traveling to Michigan with me.

This trip overshadowed the important fact that on Thursday I went to a new lawyer to sign my new will. I'm hopeful that by changing lawyers it will be easier for the boys to deal with the legal stuff after I die. I wanted them to be spared the hassle and frustration I had after your death.

I love you, Harriet

August 18 (1 a.m.)

Dear Jerry,

Yes it's 1 in the morning. I arrived about 4 hours ago and of course Kris and Dave were there to greet me as we had done for them when they visited in New York. It felt so good to see and hug them. How can I describe this relationship? It may have begun as a working relationship between you and Dave but it is so much deeper, truly soul connections. How can I not recall first meeting them after we arrived in St Martin at their vacation condo following an invitation by Dave to you during one of your daily phone calls. That was before cell phones and they really never knew if we would take him up on the invite. I'm so glad we did that and I know it was my sense of spontaneity rather than your conservative personality that influenced the decision. Thanks for accepting his invitation.

What changes they have made to their home on the lake…so Kris…beautiful, tasteful and spacious. After a tour we sat outside, had drinks and snacks and talked, about you of course and then about Israel and the Jewish people. We have always been able to talk about feelings and sensitive topics. That's part of the definition of close friends. Dave went to sleep around midnight but Kris and I continued talking just like always. I'm ready to go to sleep right now but want you to know it feels like you are here with me. You will be part of every conversation and activity I have on this trip.

I love you, Harriet

August 18 (11:30 p.m.)

Dear Jerry,

What a full and fruitful day this has been. You know there's never enough time to talk with Kris and Dave and so that's what we've been doing, but the highlight was visiting his workplace—a new plant you would have been so proud to see. He told me you had plans to visit it. Wow! Harley colors were used on the exterior and interior. The triggering moment for me was seeing the photo Dave has of you and him together, and the black kippah from your funeral that sits on the photo frame. I'm crying now as I remember the two of them helping to fill in your grave. That was a first for them as newcomers to Jewish burial customs.

After lunch Dave and I played golf and talked and talked with tears at times and laughter too, and Dave said this brings us all closer to you. He misses you so much—every day—he so looked forward to his daily call to you. 9:15 a.m. he told me, is his time to think of you. He loved you and he knows you loved him. He shared some future plans but I can't tell you right now as I am sworn to secrecy. He said he couldn't have had his success if it wasn't for you and your help. You were his mentor, his "brother" and his great friend. It is so cool that through you I have these dear friends. Dave shared about his phone conversation with our David who told Dave, "My father really loved you". Writing this and sobbing is helping me focus on my loss—so great. I notice I need to hear others speak about you and how you are missed. I think I need this as I'm usually focusing on what I had and how lucky I have been to be your wife and your best friend. I know how important it is to embrace all the feelings. I miss you so much.

Their children Katie and Brian joined us for "Shabbat dinner". They honored me with a chance to bless the candles and of course I extended it to blessing the wine and bread. They were so respectful of my ritual as they had remembered doing the same in our home when they visited us.

I wish I could hug you and whisper how special it is to be here.

I love you, Harriet

August 19 (11:30 p.m.)

Dear Jerry,

Another day filled with reminiscing about you with love and laughter, stories and tears. We shared about time with you and without you—their hearing the shocking news, the rush to book flights and get to the airport, the funeral, the Shiva—almost one year ago.

After a boat ride around the lake it was time for me to "put on my leathers" and helmet. Off I went on the back of Dave's Harley—I loved it. I felt calm and relaxed enjoying the excitement of a new experience. Memories came flooding back. I remember when you surprised me with a visit on your friend Stan's motor scooter. I was only fifteen, just months after we had met. You two had ridden all the way from Forest Hills to Laurelton. I also remember riding a scooter together again on our honeymoon in the Bahamas. And years later we enjoyed riding motorbikes while vacationing in Bermuda. It was so cool to be biking on these beautiful country roads. The memories brought smiles but I missed you on this ride today.

We headed downtown to have dinner across the street from the very hotel your dad stayed at during the snowstorm on December 14, 1936, the day you were born. David took more time to talk about his relationship with you, his friend, his mentor. He said that you and he enter his office every day together. How special is that! What a legacy!

I love you, Harriet

August 20 (noon)

Dear Jerry,

I had told Dave and Kris about the three birds circling overhead at your memorial golf tournament. This morning as we sat on their deck viewing a perfect sky, we saw three sand hill cranes flying together. According to Dave and Kris they never fly in threes, but we welcomed it as a sign from you.

It's so sad as I sit now in the airport prepared to fly home. I was overwhelmed with sadness and cried when I walked away from Dave's car. He thanked me for coming as he kissed me good-bye because he needed the time together as he had so many unanswered questions answered. And I needed the time to hear once again how special you were to Dave. Kris needed the time as well as she too loved you. Who of your friends didn't? That's why we chose to inscribe "Loved By All" as your epitaph. I cried even more when I left messages on the machines of some family and friends telling them I had such a meaningful visit. I realized I would not have made this trip alone had you not died. That too smacked me in the face, the reality of your death. This weekend solidified that you were Dave's best friend, just one more who laid claim to that title. You were "dear Jerry" to so many and still are. Remember how you would always say, "If I retire people will say, Jerry? Jerry who?" Well it never was and never will be true. You were more than what your mom called you: a 'sweet sweet soul'. You were a dear giving person and like "The Giving Tree", you continue to give and give and give. And I continue to miss and miss and miss.

I love you, Harriet

August 21 (10 p.m.)

Dear Jerry,

I opened the invitation to Josh's Bar Mitzvah today and there were no tears and no sadness, just joy and that is the theme of my response to Craig and Amy. A separate invite was there too for the brunch the next day. Josh designed it and printed them too. It is very informal but so special that he is very involved in so many ways including preparing the power point presentation of his life. I'm focusing on the excitement and plans. It may be another story that weekend especially when I see your face on the screen during the montage.

I love you, Harriet

August 23 (11:30 p.m.)

Dear Jerry,

I just returned home to a surprise message on the voice mail. Craig will be flying in Tuesday night staying only 24 hours to be here for your first yahrzeit. I believe my conversation with him last night about looking ahead to next Wednesday spurred him to recognize what he needs and that is to be with us. I told him several times how excited I was about his decision.

Today I saw three little birds on our lawn. "Three Little Birds"—you're never far away. And thank you for reminding me that "every little thing is gonna be all right."

Today I felt your absence in so many ways. I tried to "catch up" on paperwork, made many phone calls, a call to try to lock in a price for fuel this winter, calls about financial decisions, walked around the garden with Pat to reconfigure sprinkler heads, went to the bank, wrapped your wallet to be sent to Dave after he showed me the old one that you had given him for a birthday gift many years ago, sorted through papers preparing for the memorial books I'm making, reconciled bank statements, went to the dressmaker for alterations on the dress I will be wearing to Josh's Bar Mitzvah, and had a conversation with Uncle Milton who is planning to come with Aunt Shirley to the Bar Mitzvah. So many of these things you would have taken care of.

Ed came by from the office to drop off photos from The AFI 100th Anniversary Dinner. That brought both tears and smiles too.

I received a phone call from Sally before she boarded a plane in Chicago to fly home to Israel. Just one year ago, she recalled, you made a last minute change to join me to see Michael and Sally off at JFK. I remember you being so busy in the office that you didn't think you could break away. Did you somehow know that would be your last time to see them? Sally and I cried as we shared our missing you and pledged our continued love for one another.

I love you, Harriet

August 24 (10:20 p.m.)

Dear Jerry,

I'm sighing a lot (silent tears I always say). I'm working, I'm talking, I'm working, and I'm making copies for the memorial books. I'm working, I'm listening, I'm working, I'm observing. Songs I just heard on the radio: "Autumn Leaves," Embraceable You" and "Something to Remember You By".

This grief work is hard work. It is constant and it is tiring. It controls me. Who likes to be out of control? Even when I don't want to feel the grief there will be a trigger to remind me of how little control I have. I know I have control of my actions and my attitude but not my feelings and emotions. I repeat it's sad, but it's not bad. At work I led two sessions of "Coping with the High Holy Days After the Loss of a Loved One". Interestingly, Phoebe and Ed were participants and as they left thanked me for inviting them. It wasn't easy for me, the professional, to hear them publicly share their losses of this past year: his mother, her brother and "a dear friend." Well we know who that is. I kept my professional hat on.

I had planned to play golf but Florrie had to cancel so I used that time to trim some shrubs, pay some bills, bar-b-q chicken for later, welcome an appliance serviceman to fix the water dispenser on the refrigerator, confirm with Rose a lunch date when she visits from Florida and rewrite the letters I am planning to give the grandchildren for the one year anniversary. The list goes on and on and that was all prior to going to work at 2:00. I also mailed the wallet to Dave. Some of these activities are distractions and some are triggers. Everything though is helping me heal. I am sure of that. It's all about balance. How many times have I educated others to the need for balance when grieving for a friend or family member?

I know it's OK that I'm tired. I'm not depressed. I'm grateful I have the health and the strength, a healthy attitude and the awareness to do all this. Nevertheless, I'm hoping to get a good night's sleep tonight.

I love you, Harriet

August 25 (10:30 p.m.)

Dear Jerry,

"You'll Never Know How Much I Miss You" was just one of the songs I heard today that connected me with you. Another was "Melancholy Baby" and that's how I felt when working on the memory books. Reading and rereading letters, eulogies, and looking at photos has been bittersweet—happy times—but never again times. I plan to give them to the boys on August 30 when we will be together. This was 'found time' because heavy rain cancelled golf plans with Lee. I had some meaning-ful conversations with Jim, Ed and Bill today. We all know how quickly August 30 is coming.

Shelley and the kids came for Shabbat dinner and a sleepover. I went to Temple alone as it was my mother's yahrzeit. 16 years and thinking that next week will be your first anniversary made me very sad. Can it be? One year? I know I won't be sitting alone next week but rather I will be with Sue and the boys and their families. Every day has been lived to its fullest even when I have sat quietly and reflected. I know that was also doing my grief work and healing the most intense grief I have ever experienced.

The upbeat part of the day was speaking to Josh and listening to him share many of the details for his Bar Mitzvah.

I love you, Harriet

August 27 (9 a.m.)

Dear Jerry,

It's Sunday morning and I'm sitting in bed having just brought up the NY Times. It's still raining after three consecutive days. I had a good night's sleep except for being up between 12 and 1:30 so I got on the Internet and looked at maps, printed out driving directions to Cape Cod and today I will make a reservation for a B & B for the night before I take the ferry to Martha's Vineyard where I start my bike tour.

I'm flip-flopping as Louise used to say between my sadness at this time and the excitement of making plans for this bike trip that begins in a few days. I feel sad when I think and talk about you, your death, prepare memory books and then the next moment I plan for my trip, the High Holy Days coming in September and Josh's Bar Mitzvah in October and feel glad.

I'm also getting ready for the winter season; booking plane tickets to Florida through December, (planning to host another Chanukah party) tickets for the "Very Young People's Concerts" for Riley and Grant as they are now three years old, and show tickets for me.

And while many songs I hear speak to me about us, some also relate to my future, for example, "I Believe in Love" and "Love Will Be Around Again If You Will Play the Game."

I just looked at the scrap of paper on which I had written down the song titles as I was driving when I heard them. Can you believe the symbolism of my writing down these titles on a pad that had five little birds on it? You know how I always looked for symbolism even in the beautiful ring I purchased in Albuquerque. There were five diamonds in a row. To me they represented the five Vogels. Well we were five. We used to be you and me and the boys, but then Craig married, then David and Gary all leaving the nest we created. Now it's me alone, without even you in the house but always in my heart and memory.

I love you, Harriet

August 27 (11:30 p.m.)

Dear Jerry,

Cards are coming in, calls too, as people are acknowledging the upcoming first anniversary of your death. This was the weekend last year that we spent at the Galperns, the fantastic weekend with the closest of friends and in looking back you were showing signs of your heart disease. And I do believe you knew it as well.

Another rainy day has allowed me to "veg" out and make those reservations for a night in Falmouth, MA, visit with Brian and Gila on the phone, catch up on chores in the house, organize photos, spontaneously go to a movie with Marcia and follow up with dinner at her home. There are always things to do. More importantly I took time to reread my letters to you from last September to now and listen to the tape of my session with the medium, Glenn Dove. By the way Amy had a dream of you, remembering it vaguely and Craig said he experienced lights flickering when he was saying Kaddish.

"Death ends a life, not a relationship", is a famous aphorism by Morrie Schwartz written in the book *Tuesdays With Morrie.* You are so much a part of my life today. You are still so much a part of many people's lives. I know you are near. I know you will always be in my heart and on my lips. That's what I can control, my thoughts, my words, my actions, my attitude and my beliefs.

Sad is not bad! Sad is not bad! Sad is not bad!

I love you, Harriet

August 29 (7 a.m.)

Dear Jerry,

It's Tuesday, a year later. We used the alarm clock rarely as we were early risers especially on a workday. A year ago this morning we both slept late and I recall that when I woke up we had very little time to get washed and ready for work. Last night, Monday night, just like a year ago, I completed an eight-week bereavement group.

Sadly I learned it's not likely Craig will be flying in as planned because Hurricane Ernesto is bearing down on Florida and it will affect travel for sure. School is even closed for today there.

David told me he's been having a tough time emotionally, triggered by watching the U.S. Tennis Open as it reminds him of tennis games played together with you, the date and whatever else it might be. I encouraged him to "write" as I think it would help him release his feelings. He shared with me that Riley "allows" him to cry when she sees him welling up with tears. Good for her. She's learning early or is it that children naturally know what to do. It's only under the influence of uneducated or fearful adults that they learn to hold back, repress feelings, or keep silent. Open minded adults can help children feel their feelings and learn to express them in healthy ways.

I fell asleep last night listening to the tape from my session with Glenn Dove. I also made my final entry into the memory books, having been motivated by Craig's planned arrival. If he doesn't fly up I will ship it to them in Florida so they have it for the first anniversary of your death.

I noticed that I feel lighter or at least less tired than last week. So much work has been done and I am reaping the rewards.

Would you believe that the wallet I sent to Dave never arrived? The box did but the contents were missing according to the Postmaster. How fortunate that you left behind two wallets! I will send him the second one as he indeed wants a "piece of you".

Phoebe had offered to have us (the boys and me) for dinner on Wednesday before Craig's plane was to arrive and they have accepted.

On the pragmatic side I "negotiated" with the oil company for a fixed fuel price for this winter. See, I continue doing some things just like you did. You taught me so much. Thank you once again.

I love you, Harriet

August 29 (11:16 p.m.)

Dear Jerry,

If I check your death certificate it probably reads that you died about this time a year ago tomorrow night, but what are minutes when we had years together and what is a human lifetime when the universe is billions of years old? What lasts and lasts is the love we experienced.

Tonight I called the grandchildren to say goodnight. I needed to connect and hear their healing voices. And of course I spoke to Judy, Cathy, David and Phoebe as well. Each one called me. Tonight Louise's was the last phone call I received since she wanted to "tuck me in" and she says hello to you. More cards arrived today as well as books and phone messages. I've been surrounded by love and loving people.

Craig decided not to fly in with the threat of stormy winds, which may have hindered his return. I understand. I feel sad for him though.

George called and left a message acknowledging the date after attending a memorial for you at J F Braun.

I took Lorraine out for lunch as I needed to talk, and who better than a fellow grief counselor? Guess what I ordered? I ordered a half of a pastrami sandwich and a bowl of barley mushroom soup "for you" and it was delicious. I think I like corned beef better though. The song we heard driving there was "Cycles" by Frank Sinatra. Cycles of life, and the words of a song heard on the radio rang true for me once again.

Today I decided on the birthday gift for each grandchild this coming year. I will have Teddy bears made up from some of your old shirts. Fortunately I still have some having saved them to offer to David W along with dress shirts I planned to give him. The idea came when Lorraine was checking out the idea as a possibility for bereaved parents she was working with. Everything is synchronistic!!!

I lit a yahrzeit candle for you, of course, as did each of the boys in their respective homes surrounded by their wives and children. It's Jewish tradition to light the candle on the evening before the date of death as our days start at sundown. A message on one of the cards I received reads, "Rather than mourn the absence of the flame, let us celebrate how bright it glowed."

Good night. I love you. Harriet

August 30 (10 a.m.)

Dear Jerry,

I received a very special message on the phone yesterday around 12:30. It was from Tara and in her usual upbeat tone began, "thinking about you" and then it evolved into a teary voice sharing she doesn't know what to say but knew to call anyway. I began to tear up as I listened to the message while sitting at my desk. I know how hard it must have been for her to make the call as it validated why she couldn't get on the phone last night when I spoke to David. It takes courage to acknowledge death. It takes courage to acknowledge our sadness. It takes courage to cry. I'm proud of her that she had the courage to call me.

I had trouble sleeping last night. I fell asleep about 11:30 only to awaken 6 minutes later and lay there trying to fall back to sleep in vain. So I got out of bed and reread the memory book from cover to cover revisiting the obituaries, the letters, e-mails and faxes that were received after your death. I guess that's what I needed to do. Trouble sleeping???? Any surprise in that? No, quite normal, I tell myself, just as I would validate the same for a grieving client. The timing paralleled that of the phone calls I had made to each of the boys a year ago—the hardest calls I ever had to make in my life. Then I slept until seconds before the 7 o'clock alarm was to go off. That's the time I made calls the next morning to some of our closest friends to tell them you had died. Louise shared she awoke at 3 in the morning and then again at 7, the time she received my call last year.

Synchronicity at work once again! We are all connected.

I learned that J F Braun placed a memorial in Newsday and in the NY Times. I plan to buy the papers later today. I'm going to close my eyes now.

It's been raining for the last six days. Are they your tears? Our tears? Both probably.

Just received a meaningful call from Susan acknowledging the date. You were and always will be so important to her, she said.

Pepper is lying next to me comforting me like you did. I truly believe you sent her to me. Thank you again.

I love you, Harriet

August 30 (5:17 p.m.)

Dear Jerry,

Gary drove down from Connecticut and we met David and Tara and Sue at the cemetery.

Together we stood at your grave—your children, your sister, me—tears, hugs, embracing each other, prayers, placing stones each with one's own private memories, thoughts and feelings. We then respectfully stopped at our parent's graves and Sue left for home. The children and I reconvened at the Roslyn Duck Pond renamed the "Gerry Park". Was that a sign too? We had thought of walking on the beach but the weather was not conducive. We walked, talked and reflected at a familiar natural setting, a park and pond I had frequently taken the boys to when they were young.

Home to our house where I gave each family a memory book that also held the personal letters I wrote to each grandchild. The boys and Tara looked through it silently. When they read the letters I wrote to each of their children they cried as I had done when writing them. Gary and David brought their books home to share with their families. Craig and Amy will receive theirs soon, as I mailed it today. We all cried.

Sad! Sad! Sad! But sad not bad!

I love you, Harriet

August 30 (10 p.m.)

Dear Jerry,

The light still flickers on the yahrzeit candle. August 30 is almost over.

We spent a perfect evening at Phoebe and Ed's as they insisted we come to dinner at their home. Sue joined us again. We all ate, talked, laughed and remembered all the meals there through the years, especially the Shabbat after Shiva. I came home to more cards, e-mails and phone messages acknowledging the date and I just hung up with Josh. He's so special!

What did I learn this year? A colleague had asked me that question. In answering, I said, "I learned one could grieve for a close significant person without being devastated." She turned it around by saying, "You experienced what you have known and shared all these years with your clients." Sad is not bad. It's how we grieve after we've loved.

I'm reminded of the quote I placed on page one of the memory Book. It's from *Who She Was* by Samuel Friedman. "When you are sorrowful look again in your heart, and you shall see that in truth you are weeping for that which has been your delight."

I loved you and still love you, Harriet

August 31 (11:20 p.m.)

Dear Jerry,

We talked about you tonight. That is Donna, Mike and Lorraine. I hosted a party for my hospice staff, sharing my Zen garden and the history of its evolution and thanking everyone for his/ her support this past year. Earlier in the evening we toasted you, we listened to Alan playing the piano, the cats amused everyone, we laughed a lot and it felt good to entertain once again. Except for holidays, I have only hosted a couple at a time. I loved this evening as always when we had people in our home. I took your seat and thought about it lovingly. I remember August 1 and the feelings, the conversations and the anticipation of August 30 and in less than one hour it will be

September. Everything changes. One can feel sad and in time one can feel glad.

I love you, Harriet

September 1 (8 a.m.)

Dear Jerry,

The only time the sun came out all week was during a few minutes on Wednesday. David and Tara claim it did when they arrived at the cemetery and then again before my party last night. I call it symbolic. Now it's overcast with a forecast of very heavy rains tonight and this weekend, a result of Hurricane Ernesto.

I love you, Harriet

September 1 (11:30 p.m.)

Dear Jerry,

Tonight was another milestone, a benchmark of our grief journey. Tonight we all went to Temple (of course Craig, Amy Josh and Matthew did the same in Florida) to mark your yahrzeit, the first anniversary of your death. It wasn't as sad as Wednesday for me. On Monday I had already seen the plaque on the wall with your name engraved but it was the first time for Sue, Gary, Shelley, David and Tara and the friends who gathered there with us. It was sadder for them. Firsts are difficult.

That plaque will remain as a testament to your life and the connection we as a family had to Temple Sinai.

I took everyone out for dinner after services. I requested a round table at Café Picasso near the spot we had our last dinner with Howard and Helen before her death. We celebrated David's high school graduation there with a luncheon years ago. It also was the venue for my 50th birthday celebration when the boys surprised me with their band playing as the "Three V's". It was a good evening overall ending with stories and laughter.

In speaking with Craig he acknowledged receiving the memory book and appreciated it. I believe he missed not being with us on Long Island.

It's raining again and the forecast is heavy rain with strong winds both Saturday and Sunday. I prepared my clothes for the bike trip. I'll reassess what I need to take and pack tomorrow.

Good news today—two babies born to our extended family. Dan and Cori had a baby girl, Mia Isabel at 9 lb 10 oz and Elaine and Steve called before and left a message that Tracy had a baby boy today. Dave called to tell me they celebrated Luke Henry's first birthday on Wednesday as well as your life too. They will always associate your death with their grandchild's birth.

It's raining again and the rain is supposed to be very heavy this weekend, when I start my trip to Nantucket and Martha's Vineyard.

P.S. I got a notice of an Estate Tax audit. That doesn't make me feel very comfortable.

I love you, Harriet

SECOND YEAR BEGINS

September 2 (9:00 p.m.)

Dear Jerry,

Off to a later start than I had hoped for. I had gotten a flat last night on my way to Temple and the tire had to be replaced, not easy on Labor Day Weekend. I no longer started my trip when I hit a standstill on I 95 in Connecticut. I traveled only 27 miles in three hours—heavy rain due to Hurricane Ernesto. I almost thought of staying at Gary and Shelley's but at Exit 8 at 4 o'clock I decided to go for it, to Cape Cod.

Finally arrived and found my way to the B&B in West Falmouth, Cape Cod, where Tim the proprietor greeted me and showed me to a lovely room. I headed to a local restaurant recommended by him, as it was already 7 p.m. This was a first for me—eating dinner out alone. No it wasn't the first time. I just remembered having dinner alone in a beautiful country inn in the Cotswolds, England while you were dining with other businessmen in another part of the hotel. The difference is I knew I would reconnect with you after you finished your dinner meeting. The only seat available was at the bar. Like many others, I waited in line for some time just to get seated. Tim advised me it might be like that. It was not as awkward as I had imagined and made friendly conversation with the people seated next to me. The trip wasn't as tiring as I had expected either and I feel really comfortable in my nice clean bed. Good night.

I love you, Harriet

September 3 (9:45 p.m.)

Dear Jerry,

While I haven't said your name I already have had conversations with strangers about you and the fact that you died, how we made many trips, like the time we took our bikes to Nantucket, as I'm about to do this week.

However, it wasn't that easy to get to my starting point of this bike trip. After a delicious breakfast at the B & B I drove leisurely to Hyannis to catch the 12:15 ferry only to learn the ferry was cancelled due to heavy seas. I faced a challenge. How do I get to Martha's Vineyard? After investigating my options I parked my car at the Hyannis Bus Depot, took a cab to Woods Hole to take that ferry to Martha's Vineyard. I'm really proud of handling this challenge without you. I met some people on the ferry recognizing the Sojourn bag tags and introduced myself. Chris and Simon, our guides, welcomed us when we docked and the van took us to The Inn at Blueberry Hill. It was a fabulous looking classically designed wooden inn situated on several acres. After meeting more people in the group and settling in our rooms we went for a 9 mile warm up ride with weather changing from cold and rainy to warm and sunny. I chose to head to the hot tub before our scheduled orientation meeting and dinner. I shared why I chose to take this trip, mentioning you by name and the fact that you died one year ago this week. The sharing continued with lots of laughs and everyone seems nice and I'm feeling comfortable emotionally but adjusting to a new type of bike gears.

I love you, Harriet

Labor Day Monday-September 4 (5:30 p.m.)

Dear Jerry,

I cycled hard today but it was all pleasure and you would have enjoyed a day like today. It was close to 50 miles with lots of hills for sure but the views of the coastline, the sailboats, the harbors and the homes were spectacular. I don't know if I would have rated this a moderate trip though. After a 7:30 breakfast and clinic we were off. I biked alone a lot. I would have loved you by my side. While at a picnic lunch at The Wharf in Edgartown I asked a couple if I could join them as there were so many turns on this route and knowing some riders would be way ahead of me and some wouldn't go all the way. I guess I picked the right two people. We were the three that rode the whole route. It was great…I'm now sitting on my balcony with the sun still shining. The weather was perfect today after that major storm. I'm showered and dressed ready to go into Edgartown for dinner.

I love you, Harriet

September 4 (10 p.m.)

Dear Jerry,

After a fun dinner at a local pub the two other single women (they really weren't single as their spouses were home) and I went for what Simon called "power shopping" as we only had 45 minutes. You know I have a pretty good eye for finding what I like and within seconds I spotted a blue sweater that caught my eye, tried it on and bought it. In the next shop the two gals saw some more sweaters and guided me to them, decided I looked well in one and said I would have to buy it even though I was hesitant. You used to encourage me to buy clothes too so I felt your presence. When I went to pay I learned that by purchasing with my Amex card I got 20% off and was awarded a "free be"" for up to $150 on my next purchase. It paid to go shopping. We laughed ourselves silly. I always remember you joking that we were only to buy full price, not on sale, as that way we could accrue air miles for future travel.

I love you and love every time I think of things you used to say.
Harriet

September 5 (6:30 p.m.)

Dear Jerry,

We had another beautiful day, partly sunny and warm enough to wear short sleeves. We biked through a fishing village that had been the setting for the movie "Jaws". We crossed the water with a bike ferry. That was "cool" as it was large enough to carry only a couple of bikes at a time. We visited two beaches and viewed sandy cliffs. The hills were challenging for me today. I had to finish one by walking my bike to the top. I also didn't opt to do an additional 11 miles to visit art galleries. I used the van instead. Whoever said to me that Martha's Vineyard would be easy biking was so wrong. I'm dressed now waiting to join the others for dinner. Only wish you could be here too.

I love you, Harriet

September 5 (10 p.m.)

Dear Jerry,

I have not watched as much TV in the last year as I have in the last two days. It's been all about the tragic, untimely death of Steve Irwin, the "Crocodile Hunter". I watched at least four separate programs, Larry King twice, one on Channel 4 and now I'm watching Anderson Cooper. Whenever I have flown on JetBlue I watched mainly Discovery Channel and enjoyed watching this star, loving his passion and accent. His death was like your death, filled with shock and disbelief at first and then all the comments and tributes from all over the world. And very, very sad!!!!!!

I love you, Harriet

September 7 (7:50 a.m.)

Dear Jerry,

I am about to go down for breakfast but I had to write down a few memories and impressions. I hadn't done that last night because after several phone conversations I was ready for sleep. But now I'm here in Nantucket having arrived by ferry yesterday about 3 p.m. Coming into the harbor and walking onto the cobblestone street, seeing the flowers and quaint buildings I was flooded with memories of our trip here 12 years ago and realizing that *Nat Nat the Nantucket Cat* was bought here when Josh was very, very young. I also remembered how amazing it is that each of the grandchildren have loved that book and I cannot imagine how many times I have read and reread it to them each and every time they would have a sleepover. I'll write more to you later.

(11:30 p.m.) Wednesday had us all up early to place our luggage on the truck as we were ferrying to Nantucket today. The forecast called for rain so we prepared for our 15mile ride to the ferry in raingear. A few of us opted to walk around before our ride and saw the "oldest carousel" in the U.S. as well as all the "gingerbread" houses that were built by a religious order. We lunched on yummy steamers and white wine overlooking

Oak Bluff Harbor. By the time we arrived in Nantucket the sun was out for a beautiful view of Nantucket Town. I remember you and I arriving with our bicycles and duffels for a week's vacation here years ago. Do you remember walking the bikes over the cobbled streets to find the B & B where we had reserved a room? Now we headed straight to the museum for a tour about the whaling industry and then to the Jared Coffin House. By the time we got back to a stately old inn in town our luggage was in our rooms. Of course I opted to take a bike ride (I think I was the only one) prior to showering for dinner.

I saw a full moon last night and naturally thought of you and me. This morning we woke to sunshine and warm temperatures so it was a treat to walk to breakfast in short sleeves at 8 am. As our hotel dining room was being renovated we ate at The White Elephant in their private wine room. What a treat to be in this classic hotel. A great bike ride followed and on the way I bought my Nantucket pillow, a perfect souvenir I hope to keep for a long time to remind me of this fabulous week. After another 15 miles I had a chance to get into the water, bike clothes and all, at a beautiful beach. Later a cocktail party was held on the beach celebrating two couples' anniversary and then our final dinner in a private room at a lovely restaurant. It was a night of toasts and speeches and I thanked everyone for helping make this "first vacation on my own " a huge success. It's almost midnight now and I have to be ready for our final 7 a.m. 8 mile ride to the ferry.

I love you, Harriet

September 9 (11 p.m.)

Dear Jerry,

After a great week biking on both Martha's Vineyard and Nantucket, I set off to spend time outside Boston with a friend I had met in Florida, and also time with our long-time friends, Bob and Joyce, in Sherborn.

The ferry ride ended where I had parked my car and then I drove about three hours to visit with this new friend, Patty, who I had met at Harbour Ridge. A whirlwind 2 day visit included a tour of the Salem Witch Museum, where she is the director, a visit through Marblehead, its harbor and the town of Peabody, visiting an old clipper ship, dinner with other Harbour Ridge members, breakfast at a landmark restaurant, some shopping (found another pillow souvenir, this one with embroidered butterflies which are symbolic of change), and lots of talking until 3 a.m.

Driving through Peabody made me think of Rose Vogel as that's where she was from and I remembered us going to her funeral in Peabody. I thought of her married to your dad. I remembered how special she was and how fortunate that she and Dad met and married late in life after both were widowed. I thought of her wisdom and how I considered her a surrogate mother.

"You made it happen," said Joyce. "You did by calling and planning the visit."

That's what I heard when I was greeted by Joyce and Bob. I was also greeted with hugs, smiles and kisses. Simultaneously a beautiful large monarch butterfly flew by. Upon seeing it Joyce remarked, "I guess Jerry didn't want you coming alone."

Yes, I made the effort to connect with your old army buddy. We talked and reminisced and they shared their memories of your personality, your humor, and teachings. We listened to each other, learned new things and laughed and cried a bit too.

Throughout this last week there were many moments that made me think of you; you did this, you didn't do that, you would enjoy this, you wouldn't enjoy that, yet the moments weren't sad. Bob, Joyce and I went out for a steak dinner and all ordered filet mignon. However, the waiter sadly returned from the kitchen to say they were out of that cut but they could provide us with sirloin steaks prepared the same way. All I remembered is you always saying sirloin was the better steak. In addition, I tried raw clams for the first time and thought of you again but this time knowing you would not have given those clams a try. I don't think I'll do that again either.

I know for sure you were with me on this trip. You proved it twice on Saturday, once when I arrived at Joyce and Bob's. The other time was the morning I was walking through Salem. After visiting an old sailing vessel, Patty turned to me and asked if the pace was all right. I said absolutely yes but had the thought you might have found it too taxing. Yet I knew you would have loved the sailboats and the beautiful harbors. In that instant a monarch flew close to me, fluttering all around us and settled on the brick pavement right in front of us. Of course we stopped, I took a photo to remember the moment and spoke of "your visit".

There were only two times that brought tears—driving alone from Falmouth to Hyannis on Sunday morning recognizing I was doing this alone, and when Bob, your old army friend, talked about how special it is to be a grandfather and spend time with and teach his grandchildren. I agreed that the saddest times for me is thinking how you are missing those precious moments playing with the grandchildren, having one or more on your lap, pushing one on a swing, playing golf or taking one to your office.

I'm feeling tired after my first night's sleep in my own bed. Was it the six hundred miles of traveling alone, or was it the approaching anniversary of 9/11? (I had called and reached several people I had been working with and left messages for the others). Or is it the reality that I'm home where we lived and loved and laughed? And you're not here physically. This is the second year and it is supposed to be more real. I see that is true!

The first song I head when I began my drive home yesterday was "Memories of You". Thankfully, I have so many.

I love you, Harriet

P.S. While staying at Patty's home in Marblehead, MA I came across this quote by Katharine Hepburn, born 1909, (also my Dad's birth year) in a book by my bedside. "As one goes through life one learns that if you don't paddle your own canoe, you don't move."

Well Jer, I'm paddling my own kayak, pedaling my own bike, driving my own car and calling my friends. I've been making a new life for myself and I'm proud of it. I hope to continue to "paddle my own canoe" with you by my side. Where will it take me?

I love you, Harriet

EPILOGUE

I've been "paddling" for almost 10 years since Jerry died. Where has it taken me? For one thing, for my 70th birthday my children bought me a tandem kayak and I have been literally enjoying paddling on the St Lucie River adjacent to my Florida condo. To acknowledge my 75th birthday my family offered to upgrade my road bike. While that was a generous offer I opted for a new kayak, one that will help me paddle through the waters with ease. I love it. I've also tried paddle boarding a couple of times and found that fun too.

My bike trip to Nantucket and Martha's Vineyard was my first journey after Jerry died.

"Life is like riding a bicycle. To keep your balance you must keep moving."

I love this quote by Albert Einstein. In a letter written to Jerry in April 8, 2007 I included that quote adding, "I like this" and shared that it came from a book given to me by our friend

David. Perhaps I felt validated for the busy life I was living the second year after Jerry's death.

I have since traveled to Machu Picchu, Peru and The Galapagos Islands off the coast of Ecuador, both destinations that were eliminated from our travel plans because of Jerry's diabetes. After Jerry and I went on safari in Kenya, Africa to celebrate our 25th anniversary, I had hoped to return to Africa one day to trek for gorillas. I remember Jerry laughing at that idea back in the '80's. That dream came to fruition after his death as I traveled to Uganda in 2007 and thoroughly enjoyed the adventure of tracking gorillas in the Bwindi Forest National Park. In October 2014 I pursued another personal dream by visiting Bhutan by myself. I am so grateful that I had the health and courage to experience this journey, which was a spiritual and personal journey, physically challenging and a life affirming adventure.

I had an opportunity to follow up on that original hope that I would water ski with Josh and did so on his 18th birthday weekend. Each of the teenagers on the boat took a turn. Then I volunteered to give it a try so into the water I went adjusting the water skis like I had done multiple times. After three unsuccessful attempts I yelled up to those onboard, "That's enough," but thanks to Josh's repeated encouragement the fourth try had me skiing and even crossing the boat's wakes. I couldn't help but reflect on the many times Jerry and I had water-skied in the early years of our dating and marriage.

I completed the American flag afghan I had intended to knit on our trip to China and proudly presented it to Josh several years later.

I hosted my final Marriage Encounter meeting in our home having prepared the others in writing explaining that it was no longer meaningful for me to be part of the group.

In addition, I dropped my membership in the golf country club on Long Island two years after Jerry's death, another example of letting go of a life I enjoyed with him. I hold on to all the memories, though.

Songs still resonate with me, changing as I change.

Feathers still appear in the most unique places or times.

Professionally, I left the hospice agency in 2007 in order to pursue another career change. I merged my passion for hospice work with my expertise and academic degrees in education and taught "Death and Dying" and "Hospice and Palliative Care" at Nassau Community College and Hofstra University on Long Island, NY. I have maintained my private practice in grief counseling.

In 2013 I received an Honorary Doctorate from Hebrew Union College, having served the community for twenty-five years after receiving my Masters of Arts in Religious Education. While I had been a religious school educator for the first several years the majority of those years was devoted to hospice work.

Personally, almost two years after Jerry's death I joined the tens of thousands of singles who use online dating services to meet people. In the process of meeting, dating and ending relationships I learned much about myself. I continued to write to Jerry sharing this part of my life with him as well. We had been realistic about the reality that one of us would predecease the other and we talked openly about wanting the surviving partner to live life to the fullest.

I'm reminded of a passage from the book *Same Kind of Different As Me* by Ron Hall and Denver Moore. As Deborah Hall was dying she talked to her children regarding their father saying, "Your father has been a wonderful husband and father and I want you to know I'm releasing him to find someone, date and even marry. I know it's going to be hard for you, but I'm asking you to honor his decisions and let him be happy again." Had Jerry not experienced a sudden death but rather one of anticipation I believe he would have acted similarly.

In September 2011, I met a wonderful man with whom I am proud to share my life. I readily say, "How grateful I am to have had two loving relationships in my life."

Remember: "Sad is not bad. It's how we grieve after we've loved."

Believe: "Love is stronger than death. It replenishes the soul."

Family wise, the grandchildren all are well and growing. Two years after cancelling we traveled to Israel to celebrate Josh's Bar Mitzvah. I'm looking forward to attending his graduation in 2016 from the University of Central Florida.

Family and friends traveled to Florida to honor Matthew becoming a Bar Mitzvah in 2010. Matthew's love currently is golf and has played for his high school team just as his grandfather did. Graduating high school this May he is planning to go to the University of Central Florida.

This past year Jessie followed the tradition of becoming a Bat Mitzvah on her thirteenth birthday. Her sister Riley will fulfill that mitzvah on May 14, 2016, additional opportunities to gather and celebrate life and tradition as a family.

Allie has become a teenager this past January and is pursuing her talent and passion in theater, singing and dancing in musical productions. Allie and her brother Grant, the youngest of Jerry's grandchildren, play ice hockey and sail, both loves of their grandfather. Grant's golf game has come a long way since hitting his plastic clubs for Jerry during that last visit.

When our eldest son Craig turned 50, we joined together once again as a family to honor him on that milestone.

I'm excited as I look forward to our family gathering in Nantucket Memorial Day weekend to celebrate my having turned 75.

Whether it's celebrating a holiday, attending a graduation, commemorating a yahrzeit or just getting together, Jerry is always missed. Sometimes it's sad but there are other times we remember him with laughter. I am grateful for all of it.

A year after Jerry's death a memorial fund was established at

Winthrop University Hospital in Mineola NY. It is called the Jerry Vogel Pediatric Diabetes Outreach Fund. It has helped create an online newsletter called "inControl" reaching out to hundreds of diabetic children and their families. The monies raised have also helped establish an annual symposium at the hospital bringing together professionals who are working with people with diabetes and educating them of the latest information in the field by prominent researchers and practitioners.

Our son David together with his friend has raised awareness and large sums of money for the American Diabetes Association by co-chairing an annual trail run called "A Mild Sprain" in Westchester County, NY. To date this event has raised over $350,000. Tara, Jessie and Riley each bring their talent and time to assist with this huge undertaking.

Gary and Shelley now have their "dream house" and host an annual Thanksgiving dinner, which has been a Vogel family tradition.

Cycling continues to be a cherished activity for the entire family. Josh and Matthew often ride "Jerry's bike" that I had originally shipped to Florida for Craig. Craig has since advanced to a more sophisticated bicycle. Their family has taken three major bike trips in successive summers to Canada, Italy and Spain. I was the lucky one to have joined them in the Canadian Rockies four years ago.

One year I purchased four new bicycles for each of the four youngest grandchildren on their birthdays. I have had the pleasure of cycling with them at various times and places sometimes separately and sometimes in groups. I have been the "fifth wheel" with David and Tara and their girls cycling on the Bronx River Parkway when closed to motor vehicles and have ridden with Allie and Grant as well as Gary and Shelley when they lived in Denmark. I'm looking forward to exploring Nantucket by bike in May with the family.

In 2012 I sold my home of 41 years and moved to Florida full time, letting go of professional and personal ties in New York. It was a life altering experience but not as challenging a change compared to the one of adjusting to life without Jerry. Living full time in Florida has allowed me to pursue some favorite activities like golf, tennis, cycling and kayaking.

My journey has seen many changes and that includes relation-ships as well. Some come, some go, some stay and some say "no". Rarely in my counseling have I met a person who hasn't experienced the loss of one or more friendships during their grief journey. I too knew of that pain; it's disappointing and hurtful. It can become a source of anger and resentment. In the book *Tear Soup,* Grandy teaches us, "I've learned that some-times people say unkind things, but they really don't mean to hurt you."

And sometimes they forget to call or say something at all. I'm reminded of a famous quote, "People come into your life for a reason, a season or a lifetime." It's important to under-stand which it is. And it's also important to mourn that loss as well.

I continue to counsel the bereaved. Informally, I continue to support friends and family when they're experiencing grief or have questions related to end of life care. Professionally, I have been volunteering in several capacities at Treasure Coast Hospice in Stuart, Florida doing what I love; that is to support and accompany people on their grief journey. I have facilitated bereavement groups as well as visit patients and their families on the hospice program. I missed being a volunteer in the Child Life program at Winthrop Hospital on Long Island so I became a volunteer in the Little Treasures Pediatric Palliative Care Program, part of Treasure Coast Hospice. It serves chronically ill children and I have visited one child and her family for over two years.

I am developing a private practice in Palm City/Stuart, Florida as well, knowing I have the experience and the desire to help those who are grieving a loss of any kind. My website is harrietvogel.com.

With all that I have experienced and all that I have accomplished it is important for you to know that whenever hearing Josh Groban sing "To Where You Are" my heart skips a beat, my throat tightens and I begin to cry. We never stop missing the ones we loved.

Clearly I have known the power of the written word. Not only have I saved cards and letters sent to me but I also have saved copies of poems or prose I have written to others. Recently when rereading part of my collection I came across an undated greeting card I had given to Jerry. Pictured on the front was a sailboat and a bird (not joking) and the words read, "You are the most wonderful journey…(continued on the inside)… my life has ever taken." My added handwritten words were a prayer, " I pray God will continue to shower us with blessings of good health and love so we can continue on this fulfilling and fun filled journey." I simply signed it as I had on every love letter or card I ever wrote to him, "I love you, Harriet"

I know that sad is not bad. It's how we grieve after, or before, a loved one dies.

In his article called "The Trauma of Being Alive" Dr. Mark Epstein, a psychiatrist and author, writes, "The willingness to face traumas – be they large, small, primitive or fresh – is the key to healing from them. They may never disappear in the way we think they should, but maybe they don't need to. Trauma is an ineradicable aspect of life. We are human as a result of it, not in spite of it."

I am grateful I had the courage and strength to grieve the sudden traumatic death of my husband. I wish you the same.

GLOSSARY

Bar/Bat Mitzvah - literally means son/daughter of the commandments. It is a title given to every Jew upon reaching one's 13th birthday to signify that he/she is prepared to take on personal responsibility for religious actions and moral responsibility through performing and observing the commandments. No ritual is necessary. However, over the past few centuries the ritual of celebrating this life cycle event has been practiced in different ways throughout the broad and diverse Jewish community.

Bimah – a raised alter. Sometimes it is in the center of the sanctuary and sometimes up front near the ark.

Break Fast – the meal after a day of fasting such as Yom Kippur.

Challah - braided bread that is used for Sabbath and holiday meals as well as other special occasions.

Charoset - a mixture of chopped food, wine and spices to resemble mortar and is a symbolic food at Seder. The ingredients vary depending on one's country of origin; for example apples, wine, nuts and cinnamon is a traditional Eastern European recipe while dried fruit/and or citrus may be the basis of various different recipes from the Middle Eastern or Mediterranean countries

Chanukah – an eight day long minor holiday commemorating the Rededication of the Holy Temple in Jerusalem in ancient days. Other names for the holiday are "Festival of Lights" and "Feast of Dedication". Candles are lit adding one for each night for eight nights and foods cooked in oil are traditionally eaten.

Dayenu - a song sung at the Seder to express thanks to God for all God had done for the Jews. The word means "it would have been enough".

Dreydel - a four sided spinning top used to play a game on Chanukah. Each side has a letter, the first of four words translated to "a great miracle happened there". If one plays with a dreydel in Israel one letter is changed so the phrase changes to "a great miracle happened here".

Eliyahu HaNavi - a song based on the prophet Elijah commonly sung at the end of the Sabbath at the Havdalah service and during the Passover Seder as well. The prophet Elijah's message is praying for peace, hoping to "turn the hearts of fathers to their sons and the hearts of sons to their fathers".

Haggadah - the book (text) used at the Seder on Passover.

Havdalah - the religious ceremony marking the end of the Sabbath, separating the holy Sabbath and the upcoming secular week. The ceremony includes prayers said over wine, a lit braided candle (havdalah candle) and spices. The lit candle is then dipped into the wine to extinguish it.

High Holy Days – refers to Rosh Hashanah and Yom Kippur, sometimes called the Days of Awe.

Kabbalah – there are many interpretations of the word; it is part of the mystical school of thought of Jewish tradition and a means of understanding the world, life and Torah.

Kabbalat Shabbat – literally means reception of the Sabbath, and is a set of prayers either at home or in the synagogue that welcomes the Sabbath holy day.

Kaddish - a prayer praising God. It is also a shortened term for "Mourner's Kaddish" which is traditionally recited daily for eleven months after the death to remember the deceased. It is also said at particular set holidays during the year. According to Jewish mysticism the reciting of kaddish is a healing prayer both for the mourner and the deceased soul. It is interactive between the two.

Keriah - the rending of garments either by cutting an article of clothing such as a tie or blouse or cutting a black ribbon that is then pinned to a garment. It symbolizes the emotions of the moment, "the tearing away of a person from one's life". The sound alone can be "felt" throughout one's body especially in the heart.

Kiddush - the Hebrew blessing over wine, sanctifying the Sabbath and holidays. The translation literally blesses God for creating the fruit of the vine.

Kippah – a hemispherical skullcap usually made from cloth or leather worn on the head, some choosing to wear it all times and others only when praying.

Kol Nidre – literally means "all vows" in Aramaic. It is considered a declaration regarding vows made for the coming year and recited and or chanted during the evening service of Yom Kippur. It sometimes refers to the actual evening service in its entirety.

Latkes - fried potato pancakes traditionally eaten on Chanukah.

Matzah – baked unleavened bread used at the Seder and during the festival of Passover to remind us of the haste in which the Jews fled Egypt.

Mensch - a Yiddish word literally meaning "man" but used to describe someone to admire and emulate, someone of noble character, who knows right from wrong and is responsible.

Mitzvah – literally means commandment. It is also used to describe a charitable or kind act.

Motzei (Ha Motzei) - the prayer thanking God for providing bread for us. It is said before eating any meal but more commonly before a Sabbath or holiday meal.

Passover – a weeklong holiday commemorating the exodus of the Jews from slavery in Egypt. It occurs in the spring. Like Sukkot and Shavuot, Passover is a major holiday described in the Torah.

Rosh Hashanah – literally means the head of the year. This Jewish holiday starts the Jewish calendar year, generally in September or early October.

Seder – a ritual performed by a family or community on the first and second nights of Passover. It retells the story of the exodus from Egypt.

Shabbat - the seventh day of the week (Sabbath) according to the Jewish calendar, a day set aside for rest and prayer and it begins at sundown of the sixth day (Friday) and ends the following day at sundown (Saturday). There are many customs for observing Shabbat according to the different denominations of Judaism. One noted custom is that shivah is not observed on the Sabbath or holy days. Rather it is mandatory to uphold the laws of the Sabbath and holy days.

Shabbat Shalom – literally means a peaceful Sabbath and is a familiar greeting used before and on the Sabbath.

Shavuah Tov - translated it means a good week. It's a song sung at the end of the Sabbath at the Havdalah service and a greeting wishing everybody a good week, a peaceful week.

Shavuot – a holiday commemorating the giving of the Torah to the people of Israel on Mt. Sinai. It occurs on the fiftieth day after Passover and often coincides with confirmation of teens and/or graduations.

Sheloshim - comes from the word thirty ending the first month (30 days) of mourning. During this time the mourner may go back to work and normal everyday activities but traditionally is still restricted from attending joyous events like weddings. It recognizes the reality of a gradual readjustment after the week of shivah.

Shivah - comes from the word shevah meaning seven and is the period of formal mourning in the community, lasting for seven days. During that period, some mourners will traditionally sit on low stools, refrain from shaving and wear the ribbon or piece of clothing cut prior to the funeral service. The mourner will not go to work or perform chores. Instead they will receive visitors who will share memories and feelings about the dead person. The purpose is to help the mourner further experience grief reactions, face the reality of the death as well as be comforted by the visit.

Shroud – a cloth that covers but commonly refers to the garment worn by the dead for burial.

Simchat Torah – a joyous holiday at the end of the week of Sukkot. It celebrates the reading of the last portion of the yearly cycle for reading the Torah. Immediately after, the first chapter is read aloud to continue the yearly cycle of reading the Torah.

Song of Songs – a book of the Bible sometimes called "Songs of Solomon". While they are love songs between male and female lovers, it is an allegory of the loving relationship between God and the Jewish people.

Star of David - a six-pointed star and is the most common symbol of Judaism today. It is an ancient symbol and has mystical meaning as well.

Sukkot – a biblical holiday that begins five days after Yom Kippur. It is sometime called the Feast of Booths or Feast of Tabernacles. It is customary to build temporary booths whereby the roof is partially open to the sky. It is celebrated by eating in the sukkah (booth).

Synagogue – from Greek meaning a house of assembly or commonly a house of worship for Jews.

Tallit - a shawl with fringes on the bottom corners used during prayer. Sometimes it is pronounced "tallis".

Temple – This is a term used interchangeably with synagogue for a Jewish house of worship.

Torah – has many meanings, one referring to the many teachings in Jewish literature. Or it may mean a tangible object of the first five books written on parchment and attached to two wooden poles. The torah is kept in the ark unless it is being used during a prayer service. When taken from the ark it is customary to rise to show respect for its teachings and symbolism.

Unveiling - the dedication of the monument at the gravesite, usually occuring between sheloshim and the first yahrzeit.

Yahrzeit - the anniversary of the death.

Yahrzeit Candle – a special memorial candle lit before sundown on the anniversary of the death as well as the four times Yizkor is recited. It burns for approximately 24 hours.

Yizkor - the memorial prayer said four times a year, on Yom Kippur and on the last day of the three major holidays, Sukkot, Pesach (Passover) and Shavuot.

Yom Kippur – considered as the holiest day of the year, it follows ten days after Rosh Hashanah. It's a day of fasting and prayer and is one of the holy days that include a Yizkor service, the memorial service for the dead.

ACKNOWLEDGEMENTS

It was my long time friend Elaine who first urged me to "write a book" after learning I had been writing letters to Jerry for well over a year after he died. That relationship began when she had to travel from the University of Rhode Island to New York with her boyfriend Steve to gain "his friend Jerry's approval" before marrying. I thank her not only for her suggestion but also for her wisdom and unconditional love for over 50 years.

I'm indebted to the bereaved I've counseled since 1988 as I have learned from each one. I always assured them, "You are the experts, not me, as you journey through your grief."

To my friend Cara, thank you.

From the first time I shared that I was "writing a book" my grandson Josh continually encouraged me to pursue this dream. He has made it doable by sharing his creative ideas for layout and cover design, answering technical computer questions and offering helpful editing suggestions.

I am grateful for each person whether family, friend or professional who didn't judge me but rather, cried with me, listened
to me, held me in their arms or accompanied me in some way,
as I navigated "new waters." You know who you are.

And to Jerry, who for 31 years after our initial Marriage
Encounter Weekend willingly wrote and exchanged letters
with me. Thank you, I love you.

JERRY'S HOROSCOPE
DECEMBER 14,1936

Sun in Aquarius Moon in Taurus

This astrological combination gives you a steady, quiet nature that is, above all, resistant to change. Transformation and change are wholly foreign to your nature. You are a domestic person and find fulfillment in home matters. In love you rarely vacillate, remaining a sincere and faithful partner. Your thinking processes are solidly founded, and your point of view is conservative. Your level of endurance is high; only when something outrageously unreasonable is presented to you, do you display your temper. You are likely to have an active social life and good friends. Since you are content with yourself and your environment, it is no wonder that your attitude is a genuinely humanitarian one. You may be highly praised in your business or profession, because you receive such total pleasure in meeting responsibilities and commitments.